THE BEST OF
H. A.
IRONSIDE

THE BEST OF
H. A.
IRONSIDE

Compiled by
Lillian Ironside Koppin

Foreword by
Warren Wiersbe

BAKER BOOK HOUSE
Grand Rapids, Michigan 49506

PHOTOLITHOPRINTED BY CUSHING - MALLOY, INC.
ANN ARBOR, MICHIGAN, UNITED STATES OF AMERICA

Appreciation to others who helped in the selections of Dr. Ironside's writings:

My husband, Gilbert
Mrs. Sally Ironside (Mrs. John S.)
Rev. Allan and Marion Ironside Crawford
Rev. James and Enid Ironside Webber
Dr. E. Schuyler English
Marie D. Loizeaux

Contents

8 Contents

Excerpts from
The Midnight Cry

Foreword

When my friend Herman Baker suggested that
I edit a collection of Dr. H. A. Ironside's best writings,
I had to give him a regretful no. My schedule was so full
that I knew I could not do justice to such an important
project.

It was then that I suggested that he ask Dr. Ironside's
daughter, Mrs. Gilbert Koppin, to undertake the project.
Lillian hesitated for a time, but then agreed to do it; and
I believe she has done a masterful piece of work.

When you survey the large number of books that
Dr. Ironside wrote, you can appreciate the amount of
work that had to go into this project! Lillian Koppin,
with the assistance of other members of the family and
some friends, has assembled in this volume a balanced
selection of Dr. Ironside's best writings. H.A.I. was such
a versatile preacher and writer that an editor despairs of
hoping to include everything; but Lillian has given us a
hearty sampling that will satisfy and challenge the most
discriminating reader.

I give thanks that God permitted me to be alive on
this earth when H. A. Ironside was ministering. I often

heard him preach over the radio from the Moody Church in Chicago (where I was privileged to pastor for seven years), and I still refer to his books in my studies. He was one of God's giants, and yet he was the meekest of men. He was unselfish and unsparing in his ministry, and unswerving in his devotion to Christ and the Word.

Gil and Lillian Koppin are choice friends in the Lord. I rejoice that the Lord enabled them to complete this project. We need H.A.I.'s ministry today as never before, and this book will help to extend it.

Warren W. Wiersbe
Chicago, Illinois

Preface

A man of strong faith who stood firmly for the Word of God, Harry A. Ironside was always conscious of those without Christ. In teaching the Word his desire was to warm the hearts of his listeners through a simple, clear exposition. Blessed with a magnificent voice, he took command of God's Word; and young and old listened with deep respect. He was a master at using illustrations to expound Scripture. As he was preaching, his extraordinary memory enabled him to insert spontaneously a poem or anecdote he had read years before. He never resorted to notes, as the Word had been so indelibly imprinted on his mind through the power of God.

During his lifetime Dr. Ironside served as a prayer partner to thousands. Along with Bible study, prayer was a positive experience throughout his ministry and especially in the last days of his life, when cataracts rendered him blind.

Generosity was a basic ingredient in Dr. Ironside's nature; he delighted in surprising others with small gifts. There was also an impish side which many have recalled to me throughout the years. Yet he was also very humble and cringed whenever praise was accorded him. Always aware of God's goodness to him in everyday situations, he never lost sight of the fact that he was a "sinner saved by grace."

Ministers are often taken advantage of—their residences may be less than adequate; they may be bombarded by questions or other demands on their time when they need to study or simply relax. Dr. Ironside often found himself in such trying circumstances, but did his best to be kind and understanding through them all.

All the members of Dr. Ironside's family count it a privilege to have inherited his spiritual legacy. May this book be a blessing to the hearts of those who read it and an encouragement to examine more of his simple teachings.

Lillian Ironside Koppin

Excerpt from
Notes on Matthew

The Risen King and the Royal Commission

1

The Risen King and the Royal Commission

On the morning of the feast of the first fruits, the first day of the week following the first sabbath after the Passover, Jesus was raised from the dead and so became the first fruits of them that slept (Lev. 23:9-14; I Cor. 15:20, 23).

His resurrection is the proof that redemption has been accomplished. Because of His perfect satisfaction in the work of His Son, God raised Him from the dead (Acts 4:2) and seated Him at His own right hand, thus acknowledging Him as Lord and Christ (Acts 2:33, 36). Had the body of the Lord Jesus Christ never come forth from the tomb, it would have been silent evidence that He was either a deceiver or deceived when He declared that He was to give His life a ransom for many (20:28). He would have been simply another martyr to what He believed to be the truth, or else to His own ambitions. But His resurrection, in accordance with His prediction that the third day He would rise again, confirmed His claims and proved that His death was an actual propitiation for sin and that God had accepted it as such.

On Calvary, as we have seen, the Lord Jesus Christ

17

took the sinner's place and bore the judgment that we deserved. That judgment involved eternal separation from God for the wicked. As made sin, the Lord Jesus cried to God, "why hast thou forsaken me?" (27:46). Because He is infinite and we are but finite, His sacrifice and suffering were a sufficient propitiation for the sins of the world. When expiation had been made, it behooved God the Father to bring Jesus Christ back from the dead, thus fully vindicating Him from any charge of personal failure for which He should be "stricken, smitten of God, and afflicted" (Isa. 53:4). All His atoning sufferings were for others, not as penalty for any ill desert of His own. In raising Him from the dead, the Father attested the perfection of the work of His Son.

The empty tomb of Jesus is the silent yet effectual witness to the fact of His resurrection. Had it been possible to find His body, His disciples would have received it and given it careful burial again. And if His enemies could have produced it, they would have displayed it in fiendish glee as a positive proof that His prediction — that He would rise again the third day — had been utterly falsified. But neither friend nor foe could locate it, for God had raised His Son from the dead in token of His perfect satisfaction in the sacrifice of the cross. The tomb was empty on that first Lord's Day morning, not because the disciples had come by night and stolen the body while the soldiers slept (an unheard-of proceeding), nor yet because the chief priests and their emissaries had dared to break the Roman seal upon the stone that covered the entrance to that rockhewn grave, but because Jesus had fulfilled His words when he declared that if they destroyed the temple of His body, He would raise it again in three days. The resurrection is attributed to the Father (Heb. 13:20), to the Son (John 2:19-21; 10:17, 18), and to the Holy Spirit (Rom. 8:11). The entire Trinity had part in that glorious event, the supreme miracle of the ages, when He who died for our sins rose again for our justification. Joseph of Arimathea little thought of the honor that was to be his, when preparing the new tomb which was to be the dwelling-place for a few hours of the dead body of Him who is now alive forevermore.

"In the end of the sabbath, as it began to dawn toward the first day of the week, came Mary Magdalene and the other Mary to see the sepulchre. And, behold, there was a great earthquake: for the angel of the Lord descended from heaven, and came and rolled back the stone from the door, and sat upon it. His countenance was like lightning, and his rainment white as snow: And for fear of him the keepers did shake, and became as dead men. And the angel answered and said unto the women, Fear not ye: for I know that ye seek Jesus, which was crucified. He is not here: for he is risen, as he said. Come, see the place where the Lord lay. And go quickly, and tell his disciples that he is risen from the dead; and, behold, he goeth before you into Galilee; there shall ye see him: Lo, I have told you. And they departed quickly from the sepulchre with fear and great joy; and did run to bring his disciples word. And as they went to tell his disciples, behold, Jesus met them, saying, All hail. And they came and held him by the feet, and worshipped him. Then said Jesus unto them, Be not afraid: go tell my brethren that they go into Galilee, and there shall they see me" (28:1-10).

"In the end of the sabbath." The Jewish sabbath was now ended. A new era was about to begin, to be characterized by a new day. "As it began to dawn toward the first day of the week." It was the early morning of the day following the sabbath when the two Marys went out "to see the sepulchre," preparatory to taking steps for the embalming of the body, which had been so hastily laid away on the day of death.

"The angel of the Lord descended from heaven ... and rolled back the stone." This stone was not rolled back to let the risen Lord out, for He had left the tomb already. No barriers could restrain Him in His resurrection body. It was to let the women and the disciples in, that the tomb was opened.

"His countenance was like lightning." Angels are supernatural beings, pure spirits, who assume the human form at will and can disappear suddenly. "Like lightning" is suggestive of those who are said to be as "a flame of fire" (Heb. 1:7).

"For fear of him the keepers ... became as dead men." In their fright at the appearance of this celestial messenger, the hard, sturdy soldiers of the guard fainted away, unable to look upon his terrifying countenance.

"The angel answered and said unto the women, Fear not ye." Quieting the fears of the women, the angel gave them to understand that he knew their quest exactly. But he had good news for them.

"He is not here: for he is risen." This is the foundation of all our hope. It is not true, as Arnold wrote, that the body of Jesus still sleeps in a Syrian tomb. That tomb is empty. "The place where the Lord lay" bore mute evidence of His resurrection in the presence of the unruffled grave-clothes that had enswathed His body (John 20:3-8). The attention of the two Marys was directed to the empty crypt, where that precious body had reposed as it lay cold in death. No earthly hands had removed it. Jesus arose at God's appointed hour and left the sepulchre behind forever.

"Go quickly, and tell his disciples that he is risen from the dead." It was the privilege of these godly women to be the first evangelists of the new dispensation—to carry the glad news of a risen Saviour to the sorrowing, because unbelieving, disciples. Ere going to the cross, Jesus had told them, "after I am risen again, I will go before you into Galilee" (Matt. 26:32). To this appointed rendezvous the women were commanded to tell the disciples to repair, that there they might, as a group, meet their risen Lord.

"They ... did run to bring his disciples word." Love and joy gave wings to their feet as they hastened to carry the glad tidings. There was no doubt in their minds as to the truth of the angel's message.

"As they went ... Jesus met them, saying, All hail." He appeared to them Himself, so that now they had not only the word of an angel and the sight of the empty sepulchre to rely upon, but they could also testify that they had seen the Lord Himself in the body of His resurrection, and thus their faith had turned to sight. Jesus directed them to convey the good news to the disciples and to bid them to go into Galilee to the rendezvous appointed, where He had promised to meet them.

While the women were hastening to carry the news of the Lord's triumph over death to the apostles, the Roman soldiers were in a state of great perturbation over the events of the early morning, and had made their way to the city to tell the chief priests what had occurred.

"Now when they were going, behold, some of the watch came into the city, and showed unto the chief priests all the things that were done. And when they were assembled with the elders, and had taken counsel, they gave large money unto the soldiers, Saying, Say ye, His disciples came by night, and stole him away while we slept. And if this come to the governor's ears, we will persuade him, and secure you. So they took the money, and did as they were taught: and this saying is commonly reported among the Jews until this day" (vv. 11-15).

There are no depths of deceit and chicanery too low for religious bigots who are determined to pursue a chosen course to the bitter end, no matter what may be involved. When the soldiers explained what had taken place these priests, and the elders, who soon joined them, counseled the soldiers to say that the disciples of Jesus had come by night, while the guard slept, and stolen the body away.

Such an acknowledgment, if true, would have exposed them to severe penalties, but the chief priests promised to intercede for them if the matter came to the ears of the governor. They gave large bribes to the soldiers to ensure their collaboration in the matter. So they went away and gave out the story as they were instructed, and that was commonly reported, Matthew tells us, "until this day"—that is, for some years at least after the resurrection.

> "Then the eleven disciples went away into Galilee, into a mountain where Jesus had appointed them. And when they saw him, they worshipped him: but some doubted. And Jesus came and spake unto them, saying, All power is given unto me in heaven and in earth. Go ye therefore, and teach all nations, baptizing them in the name of the Father, and of the Son, and of the Holy Ghost: Teaching them to observe all things whatsoever I have commanded you: and lo, I am with you alway, even unto the end of the world. Amen" (vv. 16-20).

"Into Galilee, into a mountain where Jesus had appointed them." During His last days with His disciples, as they were drawing near to Jerusalem, Jesus had told them of His approaching death and His resurrection, and He mentioned a definite mountain in Galilee where He would meet them after all had been consummated (Matt. 26:32; 28:7; Mark 16:7). Though He appeared earlier to individuals and to various groups, it was in Galilee that He manifested Himself to "above five hundred brethren at once" (I Cor. 15:6). At least, most commentators consider this to be the case, though He evidently met first with the eleven apostles on this occasion, before appearing to the larger number.

"They worshipped him." When they beheld Him and knew it was indeed the risen Christ they were looking upon, they worshiped Him, knowing Him to be the Son of God come forth in triumph from the tomb (Rom. 1:4). "But some doubted." What a proof of the incorrigible evil of the human heart! Unbelief can be overcome only by the power of the Holy Spirit. It was some time ere all the little group believed (Mark 16:14). This helps us to understand Mark 16:17. It was promised only to the believing apostles that miraculous signs would follow and thus authenticate their testimony.

"All power [authority] is given unto me in heaven and in earth." As the obedient One, who had humbled Himself to the death of the cross, Jesus was exalted as Man by the Father to the place of pre-eminence over all things (Phil. 2:9-11). He is set as Son over His own house (Heb. 3:6), to whom all God's servants are to be subject. It is He Himself who is the General Director of the missionary program of the present age.

"Go ye therefore, and teach all nations ... in the name of the Father, and of the Son, and of the Holy Ghost." This gives the primary commission. The command is to teach, or make disciples, of all nations. The words "baptizing them" are secondary. It was not to baptize that they were sent, important as that is, but to instruct the nations in the way of life. Those receiving the Word were to be baptized as the outward expression of their faith.

The baptismal formula was in the name of the Trinity,

as was their preaching and teaching—not in the names, but the name of the Father, and of the Son, and of the Holy Spirit. Each Person of the Godhead had and still has a part in the work of salvation; therefore all are recognized and confessed in Christian baptism. The Father sent the Son, who gave His life in the power of the Eternal Spirit.

"All things whatsoever I have commanded you." During the forty days between His resurrection and ascension, Jesus unfolded to His disciples the program He would have them carry out, and gave the commandments which they were to teach to the people of all nations (Acts 1:2, 3). "Lo, I am with you alway." His presence by the Spirit was promised to all who sought to carry out His commission. "Even unto the end of the world." The last word is really "age." It refers to a time-world, rather than the material universe. Strictly speaking, the age to which He was referring will not end until He appears in glory to set up His kingdom over all the earth, but the period of the calling of the Church from Pentecost to the Rapture is included necessarily in that word "unto." During all that time from the hour in which He spoke these words to the bringing in of the Kingdom age, the gospel is to be preached, and His Spirit will be with His faithful messengers, to enable them to proclaim the message in power for the blessing of mankind.

The Great Commission to evangelize the world is not given as a whole in any of the Gospels, but we need to take all related passages in the three Synoptics and in Acts 1 to get in its entirety. There are different aspects of the commission which are emphasized in each place. Then, in addition, we have the Lord's command to the eleven as given in John 20. These all agree in this: that it is our responsibility to carry the message of grace to all men everywhere, while we wait for our Lord to return, according to His promise. In keeping with the character of Matthew's Gospel as setting forth the King and the kingdom, the commission as given here has specially in view the bringing of all nations to acknowledge the authority of Christ, and proclaim their allegiance by baptism into the name of the Holy Trinity. In its fullest sense this commission has never been fulfilled as yet. It will be completed after the Church age has ended, and a Jewish remnant will carry out the Lord's instructions preparatory to setting up the kingdom. But this does not relieve us of our responsibility to carry it out as far as possible in the present age. Mark stresses the importance of faith on the part of those who carry the message, which was to be authenticated by "signs following." Luke, both in his Gospel and the Acts, links the subjective with the objective — repentance on the part of the sinner, forgiveness on the part of God. John dwells on the authority of the risen Christ who commissions His servants to proclaim remission of sins to all who believe and retention of sins to those who spurn the message.

But all alike declare the urgency and the importance of carrying the witness-testimony, the proclamation of the gospel, unto all the nations of the world in the shortest possible time. Alas, how sadly has the Church failed in this respect! It is an appalling thought that after nineteen centuries of gospel preaching there are many millions of men and women still sitting in darkness and the shadow of death (Isa. 9:2) who have never heard the name of Jesus, and know nothing of the redemption which He has purchased by His atoning death upon the cross.

The program as set forth by our Lord has never been modified or repealed. It still constitutes what the Iron Duke (Wellington) called the "marching orders" of the Church — orders which have, however, been very largely ignored by the great bulk of professing Christians. The

first six centuries of the present era were characterized
by great missionary zeal, when, at times, whole nations
were brought to at least an outward profession of faith
in Christ. But the next thousand years, which Rome calls
"the ages of faith," but which instructed Christians rightly
designate "the dark ages," were marked, in great measure, by an eclipse of true gospel activity. With the coming of the Protestant Reformation came a new interest
in missions, in which the Moravians were the pioneers.
Later, within the last century and a half, there has followed a great awakening as to the responsibility of the
Church to evangelize the regions beyond. Today there is
no excuse either for lack of information or lack of zeal
as to missionary activity.

Some there are who deny that we of the Church age
are to act at all on this commission as given here, in-
sisting that it was intended for a Jewish testimony in
the coming era of the great tribulation. This is fanciful
in the extreme. Far more important than any quibbling
as to the exact character of this commission is the truth
of our responsibility to carry the story of redeeming love
to all men everywhere. It is given, not alone to those we
may think of as official ministers, or specially designated
missionaries, but to every believer in the Lord Jesus
Christ, to endeavor to make Him known to others and
so to win as many precious souls as possible while the
day of grace is continued. This is the first great business
of every member of the Church of the living God. All are
called to be witnesses, according to their measure. It is
ours to "go" (v. 19), to "pray" (9:38), and to help send
forth (Acts 13:3, 4) and sustain those who are able to
leave home and friends as they hasten forth into distant
lands to carry the gospel to the regions beyond (III John
6-8). The command to teach, or disciple, all nations, does
not mean that it is our responsibility to educate the

heathen along secular lines. This may come in as a by-product of missionary service, but it is not the supreme work of the herald of the cross. It is a lamentable fact that much missionary money has been devoted to founding and maintaining schools and colleges which have turned out bitter enemies of the cross of Christ. Had the same money and energy been devoted to preaching the gospel, the results would have been far different. School-teaching is a laudable profession, but it should not be confounded with gospel testimony, though it would be a happy and blessed thing if each schoolteacher were also a proclaimer of the glad tidings of grace.

The Lord's instructions never yet have been fully obeyed, and we know that not all the nations will accept the message in this age of grace; but we are commanded to go forth in the name of the Triune God, proclaiming the authority of the risen King and bidding all men yield to Him in glad surrender, and so enter into peace and blessing while waiting for His return from heaven.

Matthew closes with the Lord sending forth His messengers. We do not read of Christ's ascension here. This is significant, for it is the King commissioning His ambassadors that the Holy Spirit desired to emphasize. The last we see of Him, He is directing His representatives to go to all nations, calling upon men and women everywhere to acknowledge Him as their Saviour and become subject to His will.

When the commanding officer speaks, a loyal soldier has but to obey. The "captain of the host of the LORD" (Josh. 5:14) has said, "Go ye!" It is ours to act upon His instructions. The blessing of God has always rested in a very special way upon the individual or the church which was missionary-minded. None ever lost out by obedience to our risen Lord's command.

When we say there are plenty of heathen at home to

whom we should give our attention rather than to seek the lost in distant lands, we forget that all at home are within easy reach of the gospel, if interested in it; whereas there are untold myriads dying in heathen lands to whom the way of life is unknown, and who have never heard of the Bible or the Saviour it reveals.

There were no missionary societies in the early Church because the entire body of believers was supposed to be engaged in the great work of evangelizing the world. It was after the Church as a whole lost this vision that societies were formed to arouse interest in and forward missionary activity.

Sending out men and women as missionaries who do not themselves have a definite Christian experience is folly of the worst kind. It is but the blind leading the blind, and both are headed for the ditch (15:14). No one is fit to be a missionary abroad who is not a missionary at home. An ocean voyage never made a missionary of anyone. There must be a divinely implanted love for lost souls ere one is ready to go forth in Christ's name to carry His gospel to the heathen world. One of the first evidences of genuine conversion to Christ is the desire to make Him known to others.

It has been asked: What right has anyone to hear the gospel hundreds of times when millions have never heard it once? We may well be exercised as to this, for we are called to be *ambassadors* for Christ. This is the title Paul gives to those who seek to carry out our Lord's instruction as to evangelizing the nations (II Cor. 5:20). While our Saviour Himself is personally in heaven, seated on the right hand of the divine Majesty (Heb. 1:3), we are called to represent Him in this world, going to rebels against the authority of the God of heaven and earth, and pleading with them to be reconciled to Him who sent His Son in grace that all men might have life and peace through Him. We are unfaithful representatives indeed if we fail to respond to the command laid upon us, and allow our fellow-men to perish in their sins unwarned and knowing not the way of life.

2

Lost Ones Found

"Then drew near unto him all the
publicans and sinners for to hear him.
And the Pharisees and scribes
murmured, saying, This man receiveth
sinners, and eateth with them. And he
spake this parable unto them, saying,
What man of you, having an hundred
sheep, if he lose one of them, doth not
leave the ninety and nine in the
wilderness, and go after that which is
lost, until he find it? And when he
hath found it, he layeth it on his
shoulders, rejoicing. And when he
cometh home, he calleth together his
friends and neighbours, saying unto
them, Rejoice with me; for I have
found my sheep which was lost. I say
unto you, that likewise joy shall be in
heaven over one sinner that repenteth,
more than over ninety and nine just
persons, which need no
repentance"   (Luke 15:1-7).

All through the years of our Lord's gracious
ministry here on earth there were those of legalistic mind
who failed to understand His interest in lost, sinful men

33

and women. They fancied they were not lost; they professed to be among the righteous. They were punctilious about obeying the commandments of the law, not only that which was divinely given, but also many other commandments which had been added. So many had been added that the Lord Jesus Christ Himself said, "Ye have made the commandments of God of none effect by your tradition." They were even more particular about keeping the traditions of the elders than they were about obeying the commandments of God. They trusted in their own righteousness, and they did not realize how far short they came.

Our Lord Jesus Christ was always interested in sinners. He came down from the glory of His Father's house to save sinners. These legalists could not understand it. We are told here that a great company of publicans and sinners drew near to Jesus but the self-righteous and haughty scribes and Pharisees looked on with contempt, for they could not comprehend why Jesus did not withdraw Himself from these wretched and wicked people, and why He did not rather seek out such respectable individuals as they thought themselves to be. They murmured among themselves, saying, "This man receiveth sinners, and eateth with them." They did not know they were declaring a wonderful truth when they said that. Jesus does receive sinners, and He takes them into fellowship and communion with Himself. Thank God, this has been true all through the centuries since. Is it not wonderful grace that He receives all who will come, and He delivers them from their sins?

> "Sing it o'er and o'er again;
> Christ receiveth sinful men."

If these words come before any who have been in doubt

as to whether or not the Lord Jesus Christ will accept you, oh, let me tell you, "This is a faithful saying, and worthy of all acceptation, that Christ Jesus came into the world to save sinners!" He is interested in you; He is interested in me. I came as a sinner, and He did not turn me away. He received me and saved me, and He will do the same for you if you will come to Him.

In answer to the murmuring of the scribes and Pharisees, the Lord Jesus related the threefold parable which we have in this chapter. We need not think of three separate parables. It is the story of the grace of God pictured in three ways. The first part deals with a lost sheep in which the shepherd was interested. The second deals with a lost coin, and shows the woman's interest as she shed the light into the corners and swept the house in order that she might find it. The last part has to do with a lost son whom the father gladly welcomed home when he returned confessing his sin and failure and was ready to accept his father's forgiveness.

Jesus said, "What man of you, having an hundred sheep, if he lose one of them, doth not leave the ninety and nine in the wilderness, and go after that which is lost, until he find it?" You are all familiar with this story as it is portrayed in that beautiful old gospel hymn which Ira D. Sankey made so popular, and which we all love. You remember what it says,

> "There were ninety and nine that safely lay
>   In the shelter of the fold."

But this is not what Jesus said. He said, "Doth [he] not leave the ninety and nine in the wilderness" — not "safe in the fold" but "in the wilderness" — "and go after that which is lost, until he find it?" The ninety and nine were like the legalists who imagined they were righteous. They did not consider that they were lost, and so they did not think they needed to be sought and found. The lost sheep is the poor sinner who knew he was lost, who knew he needed a Saviour. The Shepherd leaves the ninety and nine in the wilderness, in their self-complacency, and goes out for that which is lost, and He does not give up until He finds it.

Years ago I was staying with friends who had a great sheep ranch, and one evening we were awaiting supper until the husband came home. We expected him to arrive about six o'clock, but he was late. When he came into the house he said to his wife, "My dear, I shall have to drink a cup of coffee and eat only a snack tonight, for as I came from the station I heard the bleating of a lost lamb, and I must hurry and find it before the coyotes or rattlesnakes get it." I asked if I might go with him, and he consented. I was amazed to see that man's interest in one lost lamb. He and a friend had more than five thousand sheep, and literally thousands of lambs; and yet that one lost lamb had such a place in his heart that he could not resist going out in the night to find it. I said, as we went along a narrow trail, "You have so many sheep and lambs, I wonder why you are so much concerned about one." He said, "I would not be able to sleep tonight for thinking about that little lamb out in the wilderness, and perhaps torn into pieces by the coyotes or bitten by a rattler." He called out as we went along the trail, "Bah-h-h, bah-h-h, bah-h-h, bah." He listened eagerly for an answer. At last we heard, from far down in the canyon among the thick brush, a little voice crying, "Baa ... baa ... baa." My friend answered with a loud "Bah-h-h, bah-h-h, bah-h-h, bah." He said, "There it is, You stay here; I'll go down and get it." And down he went, holding on to his flashlight; and when he got to the bottom he shouted back, "I have it; it is all right!"

We went home rejoicing together. I thought what a perfect picture of our Lord Jesus Christ searching for poor lost sinners! He knew men had wandered from God, and needed finding, and so He came from heaven down into this dark world, and He went about seeking those who were lost. Here we read that "When he had found it he laid it on his shoulders rejoicing." He did not find it to leave it and let it make its way home as best it could. Just as in the case of that little lamb of which I spoke, the shepherd did not put it down until it was back in the fold. "He layeth it on his shoulders." So our Lord does not save us, and then tell us to follow and keep up with Him if we can. He carries us home rejoicing. "I say unto you, that likewise joy shall be in heaven over one sinner that repenteth, more than over ninety and nine just persons, which need no repentance." Whatever else our friends in heaven may know or may not know in regard to what is going on here on earth, there is one thing they do know: they always know when the Good Shepherd finds a lost sheep, for He gathers them about Him and says: "Rejoice with me; for I have found my sheep which was lost."

In the second part of the parable the Lord presents the matter in a different way, in order to illustrate our utter helplessness and the need of divine enablement.

"Either what woman having ten pieces of silver, if she lose one piece, doth not light a candle, and sweep the house, and seek diligently till she find it? And when she hath found it, she calleth her friends and her neighbours together, saying, Rejoice with me; for I have found the piece which I had lost" (15:8-10).

This is a beautiful picture. One of ten pieces of silver is lost. These pieces of silver were joined together in a chain and given by the husband to seal the marriage ceremony. They were worn across the wife's forehead and valued as a wedding ring is among us. If one coin should be lost it was thought to indicate the wife's unfaithfulness to the husband. Naturally, when one of the coins had disappeared the woman would say, "What will my husband say if he should come home and find I have lost one of these pieces?" In her trouble and distress she lighted a candle and swept the floor carefully, and finally she found the coin which perhaps had rolled into a corner. She went to the door and called her neighbors, saying, "Oh, you will be glad to hear that I have found my coin which was lost!" Then carefully she put it back into the place where it belonged. It was necessary that she be active in order to discover the coin. It could not find its way back to her. In this we see the activity of the Spirit of God working through His people. We have our part in seeking for the lost. It is the light of the Word that reveals their true condition and enables us to find them. The Lord Jesus said, "Likewise, I say unto you, there is joy in the presence of the angels of God over one sinner that repenteth." "Joy in the presence of the angels." Notice He does not say what some people seem to think He says. He does not say, "There is joy among the angels," although I am sure they do rejoice; but that is not what He says; He says, "In the *presence* of the angels." Who then are in the presence of the angels? All the redeemed who are absent from the body and present with the Lord—they are in the presence of the angels. Our Lord Jesus says to them, "Rejoice with me; for I have found that which was lost." In heaven, where they know so well the worth of a soul, all rejoice when one is saved.

"And he said, A certain man had two sons: And the younger of them said to his father, Father, give me the

portion of goods that falleth to me. And he divided unto
them his living. And not many days after the younger
son gathered all together, and took his journey into a far
country, and there wasted his substance with riotous
living. And when he had spent all, there arose a mighty
famine in that land; and he began to be in want. And he
went and joined himself to a citizen of that country; and
he sent him into his fields to feed swine. And he would
fain have filled his belly with the husks that the swine
did eat: and no man gave unto him. And when he came
to himself, he said, How many hired servants of my
father's have bread enough and to spare, and I perish
with hunger! I will arise and go to my father, and will
say unto him, Father, I have sinned against heaven, and
before thee, And am no more worthy to be called thy
son: make me as one of thy hired servants. And he arose,
and came to his father. But when he was yet a great way
off, his father saw him, and had compassion, and ran,
and fell on his neck, and kissed him. And the son said
unto him, Father, I have sinned against heaven, and in
thy sight, and am no more worthy to be called thy son.
But the father said to his servants, Bring forth the best
robe, and put it on him; and put a ring on his hand, and
shoes on his feet: and bring hither the fatted calf, and
kill it; and let us eat, and be merry: For this my son was
dead, and is alive again; he was lost, and is found. And
they began to be merry. Now his elder son was in the
field: and as he came and drew nigh to the house, he
heard musick and dancing. And he called one of the
servants and asked what these things meant. And he
said unto him, Thy brother is come; and thy father hath
killed the fatted calf, because he hath received him safe
and sound. And he was angry, and would not go in:
therefore came his father out, and intreated him. And he
answering said to his father, Lo, these many years do I
serve thee, neither transgressed I at any time thy commandment: and yet thou never gavest me a kid, that I
might make merry with my friends: But as soon as this
thy son was come, which hath devoured thy living with
harlots, thou hast killed for him the fatted calf. And he
said unto him, Son, thou art ever with me, and all that
I have is thine. It was meet that we should make merry,

and be glad: for this thy brother was dead, and is alive
again; and was lost, and is found" (15:11-32).

In this third part we have perhaps the tenderest story
that our Lord Jesus ever related while here on earth. It
is a story which we all know well, and yet it never seems
to lose its sweetness and preciousness. In the first part
one sheep was lost; next, one coin was lost; and now, a
son is lost! There were two sons, and one was lost. These
two sons are typical of all mankind. Here we think of
God as the Father of spirits, the Creator of all men.
While the Word of God gives no support of the modern
theory of the universal fatherhood of God and universal
brotherhood of man; nevertheless in chapter three of this
gospel we find that in tracing the genealogy of our Lord
Jesus back to Adam, we are told that Adam was the son
of God. In this sense God is the Father of all mankind.

"And the younger of them said to his father, Father,
give me the portion of goods that falleth to me. And he
divided unto them his living." Without being content to
await the time when the father would die, the younger
son asked for his part of the estate at once in order that
he might enjoy it beforehand. The father yielded to him
and counted out to him that which was to be his. "And
not many days after the younger son gathered all together, and took his journey into a far country, and there
wasted his substance with riotous living." There he could
live as he liked, in independence of his father's will. So
he had "his fling" as we say, until all was gone. "And
when he had spent all, there arose a mighty famine in
that land; and he began to be in want." I am sure that
every repentant soul can say, "I too have wandered away
from God, and I too have squandered the good things
which He has bestowed upon me. I have lived in the far
country, and I know all that is involved in these expe-

riences." It is not a question of the amount of sin one commits that makes him a prodigal. This young man was just as truly a sinner against his father's love the moment he crossed the threshold of the door as he was in the far country. He did not want to be subject to his father; he desired to get away where he could live as he pleased. The father did not follow him. He did not insist that the son return, but allowed him to go and learn some lessons which he never could learn in any other way.

The day came when he had spent everything and found himself in dire distress. The friends he had made — where were they? They were his friends only as long as he had money. When at last everything was gone, when his fortune was spent, these fair-weather friends were not to be found; they left him in his deep need, and no one gave unto him. In his distress, in order to keep from starvation, he was obliged to do something which to a Jew of ordinary good breeding or conscience would be most revolting. "And he went and joined himself to a citizen of that country; and he sent him into his fields to feed swine." It was there among these unclean beasts, himself unclean, that he began to realize his folly and ingratitude. He could not feed upon the swine's food; he would have done so if he could. But he was a man created in the image of God who had put in him something which only God could satisfy. It is absolutely impossible for us who were created for eternity, ever to find anything in the things of this world to satisfy our souls. The day came when this young man was in such distress that he did not know where to turn. It was then that "he came to himself." That is a significant expression! Sin is a terrible thing; it is an insanity. This young man had been suffering from a mental abberation. Now he regained his right mind. He began to realize for the first time the fool he had been in turning away from the father's house, in trying to find satisfaction in the far country. Have you ever come to that place? Am I addressing anyone who has tried for years to find satisfaction in the things of this world and has never been able to do it? Oh, that you might come to yourself and face conditions as they really are, and turn to the God from whom you have wandered for so long!

This young man came to himself; he began to think. If you can get people to think then something will happen. The devil is doing his best to keep people from thinking. Some people wonder why we as Christians object to worldly amusements. They think we are very narrow and bigoted because we disapprove of them. Well, we know they are designed of Satan to keep men and women from facing the realities of life and recognizing their true condition before God. He wants to keep people from thinking, to forget they are lost sinners going on to destruction. When men begin to think they are well on the way to salvation. This young man came to that place. He said practically, "What a fool I have been, leaving my father's house and my home." "How many hired servants of my father's have bread enough and to spare, and I perish with hunger! I will arise and go to my father, and will say unto him, Father, I have sinned against heaven, and before thee, And am no more worthy to be called thy son: make me as one of thy hired servants." Oh, if any who read these lines are unsaved, would God you might come to the same decision, that you might say with the same purpose of heart, "I will arise; I will go to my Father. I will go back to God, and I will tell Him I have sinned!" The Scriptures say, "He looketh upon men, and if any say, I have sinned, and perverted that which was right, and it profited me not; He will deliver his soul from going down to the pit, and

his life shall see the light" (Job 33:27, 28). "If we confess
our sins, he is faithful and just to forgive us our sins, and
to cleanse us from all unrighteousness" (I John 1:9). That
young man, feeling his unworthiness, had determined in
his heart all he was going to say. He was going to tell
his father he was unworthy to be called a son, and ask
him to make him as one of his hired servants. But you
will note when he reached his father he had to leave out
a lot of that. The father did not wait to hear it. "He
arose, and came to his father." I have seen many pictures
of the prodigal son being welcomed by the father, but I
have not seen one which seems to be fully in accord with
the story. I have seen pictures of the father standing in
the doorway gorgeously robed and reaching out his arms
to the son, but that is not what Jesus tells us. He said,
"But when he was yet a great way off, his father saw
him, and had compassion, and ran, and fell on his neck,
and kissed him." He did not wait for the boy to get to
the doorstep; he did not wait for him to reach the house,
but he saw him coming down the road, and he said,
"There is my boy! I have been waiting for him all these
months!" What an affecting scene as Jesus pictures it.
It is the picture of God the Father. When the sinner
returns to Him, He is there to meet and welcome him.
The poor boy began to speak out, "I have sinned against
heaven, and in thy sight, and am no more worthy to be
called thy son . . ." That is as far as he got; he did not
say any more. He did not ask to become as one of the
hired servants. The father had servants enough. It was
a son he was welcoming home. He cried out in his joy,
"Bring forth the best robe, and put it on him" — for us
that robe is Christ's perfection. "Put a ring on his hand" —
the ring tells of undying affection. "And shoes on his
feet" — slaves went barefooted, but sons wore shoes. "And
bring hither the fatted calf, and kill it; and let us eat, and

be merry: For this my son was dead, and is alive again; he was lost, and is found. And they began to be merry." And that merriment has never ended. Oh, in that home, of course, the time came when the feast was finished. But when the Father wins a poor sinner to Himself and says, "This my son was lost and is found," and they enter into communion together, the merriment which begins goes on for all eternity.

But now there is an added and a jarring note. His elder brother was in the field. He is just a Pharisee, who would not dare say he was saved but did not imagine he was lost. In his heart there is no more real love for the father than there had been in the heart of the younger boy. "Now his elder son was in the field: and as he came and drew nigh to the house, he heard musick and dancing. And he called one of the servants and asked what these things meant. And he said unto him, Thy brother is come; and thy father hath killed the fatted calf, because he hath received him safe and sound." Now this brother, instead of rejoicing and saying, "Oh, let me meet him; let me have part in that merriment," "was angry, and would not go in: therefore came his father out and intreated him." He was like those scribes and Pharisees who said, "This Man receiveth sinners, and eateth with them." He considered that his father was degrading himself in treating this prodigal boy like that; one who had misbehaved as he had done! He was angry and would not go in. His father came and intreated him, but he said, "Lo, these many years do I serve thee, neither transgressed I at any time thy commandment: and yet thou never gavest me a kid, that I might make merry with my friends: But as soon as this thy son was come, which hath devoured thy living with harlots, thou hast killed for him the fatted calf." It was just the same spirit that had led the younger son to leave the house and go into the far country. This son remained at home and was more respectful, but he was no better than the younger. He actually upbraided the father for his kindness. He does not say, "My brother, for whom I have prayed so long," not "my brother," but "your son." The father said to him, "Son, thou art ever with me, and all that I have is thine." It was for him to appropriate and enjoy it all if he desired. The father reminds the elder brother of that which he had overlooked: "It was meet that we should make merry, and be glad: for this thy brother was dead, and is alive again; and was lost, and is found." The legalist can never understand the grace of God. It is utterly foreign to him.

God grant we may not fail to understand and appreciate the grace of God, as this poor disgruntled elder brother did!

3
Beyond the Veil

"There was a certain rich man, which was clothed in purple and fine linen, and fared sumptuously every day: And there was a certain beggar named Lazarus, which was laid at his gate, full of sores, And desiring to be fed with the crumbs which fell from the rich man's table: moreover the dogs came and licked his sores. And it came to pass, that the beggar died, and was carried by the angels into Abraham's bosom: the rich man also died, and was buried: And in hell he lift up his eyes, being in torments, and seeth Abraham afar off, and Lazarus in his bosom. And he cried and said, Father Abraham, have mercy on me, and send Lazarus, that he may dip the tip of his finger in water, and cool my tongue; for I am tormented in this flame. But Abraham said, Son, remember that thou in thy lifetime receivedst thy good things, and likewise Lazarus evil things: but now he is comforted, and thou art tormented. And beside all this,

between us and you there is a great
gulf fixed: so that they which would
pass from hence to you cannot; neither
can they pass to us, that would come
from thence. Then he said, I pray thee
therefore, father, that thou wouldest
send him to my father's house: For I
have five brethren; that he may testify
unto them, lest they also come into
this place of torment. Abraham saith
unto him, They have Moses and the
prophets; let them hear them. And he
said, Nay, father Abraham: but if one
went unto them from the dead, they
will repent. And he said unto him, If
they hear not Moses and the prophets,
neither will they be persuaded, though
one rose from the dead"   (Luke
16:19-31).

Before considering this solemn story concerning
which there has been so much controversy, particularly
in recent years because of the revolt against the doctrine
of eternal punishment, let me suggest two considerations
which it is well to keep in mind. First, He who related
this incident was the tenderest, gentlest, most gracious
Man who ever trod this earth. Certainly He never would
have attempted to portray human suffering beyond the
grave unless He knew and wished to impress upon His
hearers the awfulness of living and dying without God.
If there were any possibility that men might live in their
sins and yet find peace and blessing in another world,
He would have made it known. The impression left upon
everyone of His hearers who listened thoughtfully to
what He had to say must have been the same as that

which is stressed in the Epistle to the Hebrews (10:31): "It is a fearful thing to fall into the hands of the living God." The second consideration I would present is this: We have no reason whatever to look upon this story as an imaginary incident which had no foundation in fact. The question has been often raised as to whether it is a parable or not. If by parable we are thinking of a fictitious tale to illustrate some moral or spiritual lesson, I believe we are right in saying that it is not a parable. On the other hand, if we think of any incident used to illustrate truth as parabolic, then it is perfectly right to speak of the parable of the rich man and Lazarus.

In what is probably the earliest book of the Bible, that of Job, the question is raised (14:10), "man dieth, and wasteth away: yea, man giveth up the ghost, and where is he?" Apart from divine revelation there can be no satisfactory answer to this inquiry. The human mind cannot pierce the veil and tell us whether or not there be personal consciousness in other worlds than this; but in the incident here recorded He who had come from the Father's house into this world of sin in order to redeem mankind, draws aside, as it were, the heavy curtain that hides the unseen realms from view and shows us plainly what takes place after death for both the righteous and the unrighteous.

Once more, as on other occasions recorded in this Gospel, Jesus uses the expression, "There was a certain rich man." Was there, or was there not? He definitely declared that there was. He did not introduce the story by saying, "Hear a parable," as on some other occasions; neither did He say, "The kingdom is as if there were a certain rich man and a poor beggar," or some similar language. But in the clearest, most definite way He declared, "There was a certain rich man." If any of His hearers had inquired the name of the man and of the town in which he lived, dare we doubt our Lord's ability to have answered both questions definitely? He knew this man; He knew how he had lived; He knew what took place after he died. We do not know his name and never shall know it until he stands before the great white throne. Ordinarily we call him Dives, but Dives is not a name; it is simply the Latin equivalent of the Greek for "rich man." Yet this unnamed man stands out on the pages of Holy Scripture as a distinct personality, the representative of many others who live for self and ignore the two great commandments which inculcate love to God and love to man. He was "clothed in purple and fine linen, and fared sumptuously every day." He enjoyed the best that earth could give and had no interest in the things of eternity.

Next we are told that "there was a certain beggar named Lazarus, which was laid at his gate, full of sores, and desiring to be fed with the crumbs which fell from the rich man's table: moreover the dogs came and licked his sores." This poor beggar is mentioned by name because the Good Shepherd "calleth his own sheep by name." In spite of his wretched circumstances, Lazarus (which means "God is my help") was a man of faith, a true son of Abraham. Had conditions been right in Israel no son of Abraham would have been found in such a plight, but Lazarus was suffering because he was part of a nation that had drifted far from God and had forfeited all right to claim His temporal mercies, mercies which were promised to the nation if obedient to the divine law. Apparently the rich man felt no concern whatever for this poor beggar who was daily brought to his gate by friends or relatives with the hope that Lazarus might receive sufficient alms to nourish him and prolong his life. He seems to have been passed by with contemptuous indifference. The dogs showed more concern for him than his own kind who thought only of gratifying their selfish desires.

But at last a great change came. The beggar died and was carried by the angels into Abraham's bosom. Possibly Dives and his associates did not even hear of the death of this man. We have no record of a funeral service. The poor, wretched, starved body was thrown, perhaps into the continual fires burning in the valley of Hinnom, or left to be devoured by hyenas or jackals; or if there were someone who was sufficiently interested to give it a burial it must have been of the simplest possible character. And yet as we look beyond the veil, enabled to do so by our Lord's words, we see a convoy of angels waiting to conduct the spirit of this erstwhile poverty-stricken wretch into the bosom of Abraham, the father of the faithful. It is distinctly a New Testament revelation that when believers die now they depart to be with Christ which is far better; but before the cross the highest hope of the godly Hebrew was to be welcomed by Abraham, with whom the covenant had been made, into an abode of bliss. We should not make the mistake of thinking of Abraham's bosom as the name of a locality in Hades. The locality was paradise. Abraham's bosom was the bosom of Abraham. In other words, Abraham, a living person, even though his body was long since dead, welcomed to that abode of happiness this child of faith when he moved out of his afflicted body.

We are not told how soon after the death of Lazarus the rich man also died, but it could not have been very long. We read that he "was buried." That, in itself is significant. Undoubtedly he had a great funeral service with many hired mourners and every possible honor paid to the lifeless clay that had once housed his selfish spirit, but while the funeral service was being held on earth, he himself, the real man, was in hell enduring the torments of the damned.

I know that many today will object to this. Some will cry out, "Stop a moment. The word translated *hell* there does not refer to the final abode of the lost which is really Gehenna," and we grant that. They insist that Hades does not convey any thought of judgment to come. But let us read the passage again and use the Greek word and see how it sounds. "The rich man also died, and was buried: And in *Hades* he lift up his eyes, being in torments." Observe that "torments" was not done away with by changing the word from English to Greek. Others insist that Hades, after all, does not mean the "world of the lost"; it simply means "the grave," and should be so translated. While we do not for a moment accept this view, let us read it that way and see if it helps us to escape the apparent teaching of the story: "the rich man also died, and was buried: And in *the grave*, he lift up his eyes, being in torments." Notice that the torment is still there even though we have changed the word so drastically. Was the man buried alive that he suffered torments in the grave? No; we are told he died, and after he died, in another world than this, he suffered torments.

Next we learn two remarkable things: First, that spirits out of the body are perfectly conscious and able to converse one with another. Second, that there is recognition in the unseen world. There is recognition of the redeemed in paradise by the lost who are in hell, even though between the two there is a great gulf fixed.

As we pursue the story we see that the separation which takes place in the hour of death remains for all eternity. Dives looked up in his torment and saw Lazarus in Abraham's bosom. That lost man looked into paradise and there he beheld what he had missed. He saw what would have been his if only he had given God His rightful place in his life: he saw the one who had lived as a neglected beggar at his gate, now enjoying a bliss which he himself would never know. In his distress he began to pray. Think of that—a praying man in hell! But the trouble is he began to pray on the wrong side of the tomb. While on earth he felt no need of prayer; he lived his own self-centered life in utter indifference to the claims of God and man. But in eternity he began to pray when prayer was useless. He did not ask for much at first, simply a drop of cold water on the tip of the beggar's finger, but even that was denied him. He used the language of the physical although it was spiritual thirst— a thirst which he never would have known if he had availed himself of the offer to drink of the living water while he was on earth. Now it was too late. Abraham, to whom the prayer was addressed, replied, "Son, remember that thou in thy lifetime receivedst thy good things, and likewise Lazarus evil things: but now he is comforted, and thou art tormented." Son, remember! What a terrible thing memory will be for the unsaved: to remember throughout all eternity every sin committed and unrepented of, and therefore unforgiven; to remember every opportunity to get right with God which had been carelessly passed by; to remember every gospel message one has ever heard and yet refused to believe. Memory will be indeed as the worm that dieth not, tormenting the soul forever.

Abraham's words show that one might have on earth everything the heart could desire and have nothing for eternity. On the other hand, one might seem to have nothing on earth to minister to his need and comfort, and yet have everything for the world to come.

Then the words that follow tell us of the impossibility of any change throughout the ages to come. "And beside all this, between us and you there is a great gulf fixed: so that they which would pass from hence to you cannot; neither can they pass to us, that would come from thence." A great gulf fixed! The separation of the saved and the lost is final when one has passed through the gate of death into worlds unseen. Here is the death-blow to universalism. Naturally we would like to believe that there is some way by which those who have died without repenting of their iniquities, might be cleansed from their sins, even after ages of suffering, and enjoy the beatific vision, but the gulf is impassable. The saved can never lose their blessing and fall into perdition; the lost can never attain to blessing and enjoy salvation.

Hopeless of any alleviation of his own misery, the rich man suddenly became missionary-minded. Pitifully he pleaded for his five brothers still on earth and begged that Lazarus might be sent to them from the dead to warn them, so that they might not come to that same place of torment. We have heard unsaved people flippantly exclaim at times, "Well, if I am lost I shall have plenty of company in hell." We have no suggestion here of anything like that. This man does not desire company; he does not want his most intimate relatives to be there. It gives us some conception of the awful loneliness of hell. Even if one should be conscious of the nearness of those whom he had known on earth it would only add to his wretchedness.

Think of the family to which this man belonged: there were six brothers, one was in hell and five were on the way! Yet for all of them Christ had come to die. They need not have been lost if they had been ready to receive the message of grace.

This second prayer, like the former, had to go unanswered. Abraham replied, "They have Moses and the prophets; let them hear them." That is to say, they have

God's Word; they have their Bibles; let them read the Word; let them heed what they find therein, and they will never know the meaning of a lost eternity. But if they refuse the Word then not even a man coming back from the dead could persuade them to repentance. Dives reasons otherwise. He exclaimed, "Nay, father Abraham: but if one went unto them from the dead, they will repent." The answer comes back sternly in the negative, "If they hear not Moses and the prophets, neither will they be persuaded, though one rose from the dead." The man who refuses to heed the clear, definite instruction of the Holy Scriptures would never believe though one came to him asserting that he had been on the other side of the tomb and had returned to warn him to flee from the wrath to come.

Surely no thoughtful person can read this story seriously without realizing that our Lord Jesus meant us to understand that if we die in our sins, if we go out of this world loving the things which God hates and hating the things which God loves, we must be separated from Him forever.

But now another consideration ere we close this message. If this story be only a parable, as some tell us, what is it meant to teach? The answer given by materialists of different groups who deny the consciousness of man after death and refuse the doctrine of eternal retribution for sin, is ordinarily something like this: The rich man, we are told, pictures the Jewish people who in centuries gone by enjoyed all the blessings of God and kept them selfishly to themselves; the poor man, despite his Jewish name, represents the Gentiles who were strangers to the covenants of promise but lay, as it were, outside the door of the favored Jew. A new dispensation is represented by their death. Now it is the Gentile who is in the place of privilege, even in Abraham's bosom, having become an heir to the promises to which before he had no claim. The Jew is the outcast now, and has been suffering all down through the centuries because of the sins of his fathers. At first this seems plausible enough, but now let us go a step further. This outcast Jew and this highly privileged Gentile—are they separated by a gulf that cannot be passed? Is it true tht the Jew cannot come from his present place of suffering into the privileges of Christianity? Is it also true that the favored Gentile cannot refuse the grace of God in Christ and go over, if he will, to the place in which the Jew himself is found? Surely not. No such gulf has ever been fixed on earth. Any Jew may accept Christ and enter into all the blessedness of gospel light and privilege; and any Gentile who refuses the grace of God passes over to the place in which the unsaved Jew is found under the judgment of God.

The only legitimate deduction therefore is that our Lord related this incident to bring clearly before us the importance of being right with God in this world in order that we might enjoy His favor in the world to come.

The Prophet Isaiah

The Suffering Saviour

4
The Suffering
Saviour

The inspired writer gives us a graphic pen-por-
trait of the suffering Saviour and tells us of the glorious
work He was to undertake in order that the sin question
might be settled forever to the perfect satisfaction of
God, the infinitely Holy One.

This great Messianic prophecy is referred to a number
of times in the New Testament, and in each instance is
applied directly to our Lord Jesus Christ, as in Matthew
8:17; Acts 8:32-35; and I Peter 2:21-25.

Christ is here presented as the sinless Substitute for
sinful men, to whom our sins were imputed that divine
righteousness might be imputed to us who believe in
Him. His lowly life, His rejection by His own people, His
voluntary subjection to the suffering of the Cross, His
atoning sacrifice, His glorious resurrection and the
triumph of His gospel in the salvation of a great host of
sinners are all foretold here in a clear and concise way.
None but God Himself could have given us this remarkable delineation of the character and work of the Lord
Jesus so long before He came into the world. Isaiah
wrote this prophecy some seven hundred years before

Jesus was born in Bethlehem in order to fulfill all that was written of Him. God foreknew all that His Son was to endure, and He gave this message to Isaiah to hand on to the future generations.

This wonderful passage begins with the 13th verse of chapter fifty-two: "Behold, my servant," for the One whom it describes is the same Person of whom he continues to speak in chapter fifty-three.

This is Hebrew poetry in blank verse, as may be seen from various other versions and translations. It is in sections of three stanzas each. The first one (52:13-15) introduces the Servant of Jehovah whose glory must be equal to the shame He endured.

> Behold, my servant shall deal prudently, he shall be exalted and extolled, and be very high. As many were astonied [astonished] at thee; his visage was so marred more than any man, and his form more than the sons of men: So shall he sprinkle many nations; the kings shall shut their mouths at him: for that which had not been told them shall they see; and that which they had not heard shall they consider.

Hebrew scholars tell us that the word "sprinkle" here is from the same root as that for "astonied," so that it really means, As many were astonished at Him, so shall He astonish many nations.

Then chapter fifty-three presents God's servant, the suffering Saviour.

> Who hath believed our report? and to whom is the arm of the LORD revealed? For he shall grow up before him as a tender plant, and as a root out of a dry ground: he hath no form nor comeliness; and when we shall see him, there is no beauty that we should desire him. He is despised and rejected of men; a man of sorrows, and acquainted with grief: and we hid as it were our faces

from him; he was despised, and we esteemed him not
(vv. 1-3).

To the question, "Who hath believed our report?"
Paul the apostle calls our attention in Romans 10:16 as
evidencing the incredulity of Israel, the very people who
had waited for the coming of their Messiah for centuries,
but who, when He came, fulfilled their own Scriptures
in rejecting Him. They failed to see in Jesus "the arm
of the LORD" stretched forth for their salvation, as in the
case of the great bulk of mankind today.

Christians often say that in their unconverted days,
the Lord was to them as a root out of a dry ground, but
now He is the altogether lovely one. But the expression
does not imply lack of comeliness or beauty, but that
the Lord Jesus Christ grew up before God as a sprout,
a root. This is the Man whose name is "the Branch," a
root out of the dry ground of formalistic Israel, the one
lovely plant that Jehovah gazed down upon with such
approval that He could open the heavens above Him and
say, "This is My beloved Son, in whom I have found [all]
My delight" (Darby). This was what the blessed Lord
was to God—a tender plant, a plant of renown and beauty,
growing out of the dry ground of Israel and of humanity
in general. To God He was precious beyond words, but
to unbelieving men He had no form, no comeliness, no
beauty; that is, men did not recognize the moral loveliness that He ever exhibited. Some Christian teachers
have misunderstood the expression, "He hath no form
nor comeliness," and have believed that the Lord Jesus
Christ as man was positively repulsive in appearance, so
that no one would like to look upon Him. But that is
not in accordance with other scriptures.

In Psalm 45:2 it is written of our blessed Lord, "Thou
art fairer than the children of men," and we have every

reason to believe that the Lord Jesus Christ, being the only sinless child that was ever born into the world, came here with a perfect human body and spotlessly beautiful. And as He grew up as a young man and later matured, He would be of lovely, splendid appearance, but those who listened to His teaching but loved their sins, and were angered by Him, saw in Him no beauty that they should desire Him.

It is not a question of physical characteristics; because of the sufferings He endured, His visage became marred more than any man, and His form more than the sons of men. But as Man here on earth, the Second Man, the Last Adam, He was as to His human form, face, and features absolutely perfect. But men looked upon Him with scorn and disdain because His teaching interfered with the lives that they loved to live. They say, "When we shall see him, there is no beauty that we should desire him."

So the prophet goes on to say:

> He is despised and rejected of men; a man of sorrows, and acquainted with grief: and we hid as it were our faces from him; he was despised, and we esteemed him not (53: 3).

All this was fulfilled in the days of our Lord's ministry here on earth. Before that there is no hint that he was despised and rejected. The little that we are told of Him is that "Jesus increased in wisdom and stature, and in *favour* with God and man" (Luke 2:52). Before His ministry began, He must have been acceptable wherever He went; He was evidently a reader in the Nazareth synagogue because He went there and publicly began to read from this very book of Isaiah, so that He was in favor in the eyes of His townsmen.

It was when He went out on His great mission that men turned away from Him—despised and rejected Him—a man of sorrows and acquainted with grief, and we hid as it were our faces from Him; He was despised and we esteemed Him not. Yet He was suffering in our place. Rejected, despised, He endured patiently all the shame put upon Him.

> Surely he hath borne our griefs, and carried our sorrows: yet we did esteem him stricken, smitten of God, and afflicted (v. 4).

Men looked upon the sorrows He endured as divine judgments for His own sins, deserved because of what He was in Himself, as though God was angry with Him, whereas He was but entering into our griefs and the sorrows that sin had brought upon the race of mankind. All through His lowly life He saw what misery sin had caused. Men said He had a devil, and called Him a Samaritan—made Him out as a deceiver, and considered that the sufferings that He endured were deserved.

> But he was wounded for our transgressions, he was bruised for our iniquities: the chastisement of our peace was upon him; and with his stripes we are healed. All we like sheep have gone astray; we have turned every one to his own way; and the LORD hath laid on him the iniquity of us all (v. 5, 6).

This brings us to the Cross, where He endured vicariously the judgment that our sins deserved in order that through His stripes we might be healed. There on the tree He was the great sin offering and the peace offering, too—there He "made peace through the blood of His cross" (Col. 1:20).

Surely here is substitutionary atonement. Sometimes

people object to this on the ground that the word "substitution" is not found in the Bible, but when one is in the place of another, when one is taking what another deserves, that is substitution, and here we have the plain, definite statement, "He hath borne our griefs ... he was wounded for our transgressions, he was bruised for our iniquities," the chastisement whereby our peace was made fell upon Him with the result: "with his stripes we are healed."

In verse six God, as it were, balances the books of the world—two debit entries and one credit entry. The two debit entries: "All we like sheep have gone astray"—there is the whole fallen human race; "we have turned every one to his own way"—there is each individual's own personal sin; and then the credit entry that clears it all on the books of God if men would but receive it: "the LORD hath laid on him the iniquity of us all."

Here we have the entire story of the Bible epitomized: Man's ruin both by nature and practice, and God's marvelous and all-sufficient remedy. The verse begins with *all* and ends with *all*. An anxious soul was directed to this passage and found peace. Afterward he said, "I bent low down and went in at the first *all*. I stood up straight and came out at the last." The first is the acknowledgment of our deep need. The second shows how fully that need has been met in the Cross of Christ. How happy to be numbered among those who have put in their claim and found salvation through the atoning work which there took place!

To me verse six is the most wonderful text in the Bible. I have been trying to preach for sixty years and that is the first text I ever preached on. I was just a boy fourteen years old, and out on the street in Los Angeles with the Salvation Army, I started speaking on that verse, meaning to take five minutes, but a half-hour later the captain leaned over and said, "Boy, we should have been in the Hall twenty minutes ago. You'll have to tell us the rest some other time." I have been trying to tell the rest all through the years since, but it is a text I never get beyond.

The mock trial of the Lord is next foretold.

Excerpts from

Notes on the Minor Prophets

5

A Brand Plucked Out
of the Fire

The fourth vision may be looked at in two ways. Primarily it sets forth Israel's cleansing, judicially and morally, in the last days. It is also a lovely gospel picture, which the soul delights to dwell upon.

Joshua the high priest, the associate of Zerubbabel, the uncrowned heir of David's line, is seen standing before the angel of Jehovah, as if for judgment. At his right hand appears Satan, the adversary, ever the accuser of the people of God. But he is not permitted to raise any question, or to bring any charge, though Joshua is clothed in filthy garments; for the Lord Himself speaks, saying, "The LORD rebuke thee, O Satan; even the LORD that hath chosen Jerusalem rebuke thee; is not this a brand plucked out of the fire?" (Zech. 3:1-3).

It is strikingly solemn, and yet a lovely scene. Joshua represents the entire remnant company; for as priest he went in to God on their behalf. But he is clothed, not in the unsullied robes prescribed by the law, but in filthy garments — setting forth the moral pollution of the whole nation. Isaiah's description well accords with this significant picture, "Why should ye be stricken any more?

69

ye will revolt more and more: the whole head is sick, and the whole heart faint. From the sole of the foot even unto the head there is no soundness in it; but wounds, and bruises, and putrifying sores: they have not been closed, neither bound up, neither mollified with ointment" (Isa. 1:5, 6).

Constitutionally corrupt, the filth of Judah's pollution defiled all her garments, and made them filthy and vile in God's sight. Who would have supposed any people so unclean could have been accepted of Jehovah? Surely the adversary would find ready ear when he sought to prefer his charges before the throne of infinite holiness! But God had taken into account all Israel's failures when He first took them up in grace, so He will listen to no charge against them. He rebukes the devil with the declaration that He has chosen Jerusalem, and that Joshua, as the people's representative, is a brand plucked out of the fire. This is matchless lovingkindness surely, but just what we should expect here; for "the gifts and calling of God are without repentance." He will chasten and discipline his failing people, but He will not allow Satan to prefer a single charge against them, for provision has been made for their moral fitness for His presence. Zechariah then hears Jehovah's voice saying to those who stood before Him, "Take away the filthy garments from him." While to Joshua himself the word is given, "Behold, I have caused thine iniquity to pass from thee, and I will clothe thee with change of raiment"(Zech. 3:4).

At this the prophet's soul was stirred to its depths, and, entering into the spirit of the occasion, he cried out, "Let them set a fair mitre upon his head!"

Immediately it is done as he requested, and as God had commanded. So Joshua appears no longer as a type, or symbolic character, of Judah, polluted by her failures and sins, but of the remnant which shall be regenerated in the day of Jehovah's power, when she shall be cleansed from all her pollutions and He will be pacified toward her for all that she has done (Ezek. 16:60-62).

No more beautiful gospel picture is found within the Bible covers than this. As aptly as Joshua stands for Judah, so does he represent the poor sinner coming into God's holy presence with all his guilt upon him. It is thus every soul must meet Him for the first time. None can put away his iniquity and thereby fit himself to face that righteous throne. But clad in his filthy garments, owning fully all his dreadful guilt, every repentant soul may approach God with the conscious knowledge that for such as he there is mercy and cleansing.

The adversary will be there to hinder if he can; but Jehovah will not listen to him, for He has His eye on the work of the Lord Jesus Christ, accomplished on Calvary's cross, when "he bare the sin of many, and made intercession for the transgressors" (Isa. 53:12). Against that mighty intercession no Satanic charges can avail. Too loudly cries the blood in God's ear that speaketh better things than that of Abel. Therefore of every believing sinner He delights to say, "is not this a brand plucked out of the fire?"

Nor is it merely judicial clearance, but there will be moral fitness too; for those whom God justifies He likewise cleanses, purifying their hearts by faith, when they are born of the water of the Word and by the Spirit of holiness.

Thus are God's redeemed ones called to serve Him whose grace has plucked them as brands from eternal fire. And so, in the coming age, will restored and purged Israel delight to obey the voice of Him who shall have made them willing in the day of His power.

Only in Christ shall all these prophetic pictures be made good; so at once we are told, "I will bring forth

my servant the BRANCH" (v. 8). The title is not a new
one as applied to the Lord Jesus. Again and again had
the older prophets so designated Him. Isaiah more than
once foretold the day when "the Branch of the LORD"
should be for beauty and for glory (Isa. 4:2; 11:1); and
Jeremiah twice spoke of David's righteous Branch, who
was to be called Jehovah Tsidkenu (Jer. 23:5, 6; 33:15, 16).
So Zechariah but amplifies here and in chapter 6:12 what
God had long before made known.

6

The Four Chariots and the Crowning Day

This chapter concludes the first division of the prophecy, and is itself divided into two parts. Verses 1 to 8 of chapter 6 give us Zechariah's final vision. Verses 9 to 15 set forth the glorious climax of all prophetic instruction, in figure; the crowning of Joshua the high priest representing the coronation of our Lord Jesus Christ when He shall be manifested to Israel as "a Priest forever, after the order of Melchizedek," who combined in himself the kingly and priestly offices.

The vision is simple, yet comforting, and requires but little explanation. Zechariah saw four chariots, drawn respectively by red, black, white and speckled bay horses. No mention is made of drivers. It would seem as though the horses were directed by unseen agency, which is fully in keeping with the explanation given afterward.

The chariots and their horses were seen coming out from between two mountains of brass. The prophet inquired as to the identity of the symbols, and was answered by the angel, who said, "These are the four spirits of the heavens, which go forth from standing before the Lord of all the earth. The black horses which are therein go forth into the north country; and the white go forth after them; and the grisled go forth toward the south country. And the bay* went forth, and sought to go that they might walk to and fro through the earth." Then the angel addressed the restless steeds directly, bidding them, "Get you hence, walk to and fro through the earth."

At once they started on their mission, whereupon the angel turned again to Zechariah, and said, "Behold, these that go toward the north country have quieted my spirit in the north country" (vv. 1-8).

The vision evidently sets forth God's control of all destructive agencies used by Him in the punishment of the nations that have deserved His wrath. It was intended to give repose of heart and confidence of mind to the remnant, making known to them the fact that the God of Israel was the Lord of all the earth. "All things serve his might." In His own way and time, therefore, He would send the chariots of His government against the nations that had made a prey of and spoiled His people. "Mountains of brass" (v. 1) speaks of power in righteous judgment. From between two such mountains the chariots go forth.

God's providential agencies may seem, to unbelief, like restless, uncurbed horses rushing here and there according to blind chance or their own uncontrolled energy. But the man of faith, though he cannot always see the Hand that guides the reins, yet knows that divine wisdom orders all according to righteousness.

The special prophetic application of what Zechariah had beheld was at that moment connected with the kingdom of Babylon on the north and Egypt on the south. Between these two powers God would sustain His feeble flock, checkmating every effort to destroy them till Mes-

*Some read, "the red;" see RV, margin. Others translate this word, "the strong."

siah should Himself appear. Alas, that when He came
they knew Him not! Therefore they have been driven from
their ancestral home and scattered among the Gentiles.
But in the last days they will again be found in a similar,
though more serious, state than that in which they once
failed so grievously. Then the lesson of this vision will
be for their comfort and cheer, bidding them look up in
confidence to Him who controls all agencies that would
seek their overthrow. Compare Revelation 7:1-3, where
four angels are seen holding the winds, or spirits of destruction, in check till the sealing of the remnant who
are to be preserved for the kingdom soon to be
established.

We have thus gone over the apocalypse of Zechariah,
seeking to understand his visions in their prophetic and
moral bearing. They harmonize perfectly with those of
Daniel and the Revelation, as also with the unfolding of
the ways of God in Hosea.

We are now to notice a symbolic action on the part
of the prophet, which sets forth the bringing in of the
glory, or the crowning day—the coronation of the once-
rejected Jesus as Priest-King over all the earth.

Zechariah was bidden to go to some of the returned
captivity, and to take from them gifts of silver and gold
to make crowns. One he was directed to set upon the
head of Joshua the son of Josedech, the high priest; but
even as he did so, he was to speak of a greater than
Joshua, saying, "Behold the man whose name is The
BRANCH; and he shall grow up out of his place, and he
shall build the temple of the LORD: Even he shall build
the temple of the LORD; and he shall bear the glory, and
shall sit and rule upon his throne; and he shall be a priest
upon his throne: and the counsel of peace shall be between them both" (vv. 12, 13).

Upon the brows of the associates of Joshua crowns

were also placed, as setting forth the dignity of restored Israel when they shall all be a kingdom of priests. This was done "for a memorial in the temple of the LORD" (v. 14). Then followed a declaration that "they that are far off shall come and build in the temple of the LORD, and ye shall know that the LORD of hosts hath sent me unto you. And this shall come to pass, if ye will diligently obey the voice of the LORD your God" (v. 15).

Those directly addressed by Zechariah did not diligently obey Jehovah's voice, and so forfeited the promised blessing. But in a future day an obedient remnant will be found who shall be born again, and in whose hearts and minds will be written the law of God so that they shall delight in His testimonies. Then shall the Branch of Jehovah be glorious throughout the whole earth, and the crown be placed upon that brow that was once pierced with the mock crown of thorns, when Pilate led Him forth, uttering unconsciously the very words of the prophet, "Behold the man!" There he stopped, for the hour had not yet come when that lowly Man was to be invested with His regal glories. But when God brings His First-begotten into the world again, He will call upon all created intelligences, human and angelic, to do Him homage. Then shall the promise of the 110th psalm be fulfilled, and His Melchizedek priesthood, in relation to Israel and the earth, be ushered in.

The words, "he shall build the temple of the LORD," together with the prophecy of verse 15, make it clear that another and more glorious temple than that of Zerubbabel was contemplated. That house, "exceeding magnifical," is fully described, together with its surroundings and order, in the last eight chapters of Ezekiel. It is to be built when the long-looked-for King has come, and in His Person the two offices of Priest and Ruler combine.

"The counsel of peace shall be between them both," we are told. That is, the new covenant will rest, not on an agreement entered into by man and God, but it will be established forever on the ground of "the counsel of peace" made between Jehovah of hosts and the Man whose name is "The BRANCH." He, the Man of God's purpose, settled every question as to sin when He died upon the tree; and now, "having made peace through the blood of his cross," He is the agent through whom the reconciliation of all things in heaven and earth will be effected (Col. 1:20).

Thus have we been carried in spirit from the days of Judah's first restoration to her final blessing in the land, when "this man shall be the peace," (Mic. 5:5) and "in his times he shall shew, who is the blessed and only potentate, the King of kings, and Lord of lords" (I Tim. 6:15). This is the ultimate goal of prophecy.

7
Bands of Love

"When Israel was a child, then I loved him, and called my son out of Egypt" (Hos. 1:1). It is plain, from a consideration of Matthew 2:15, that God had in view His own Son, our Lord Jesus Christ, when the prophet uttered these words. Clearly, and unmistakably, the Holy Babe's sojourn in the land of Egypt is declared to be, "that it might be fulfilled which was spoken *of the Lord* by the prophet, saying, Out of Egypt have I called my son."

And yet a careful reading of the first few verses of Hosea 1 will make it equally clear that the prophet himself, doubtless, had none other than Israel nationally before him when he spoke the words quoted. He was dwelling on Israel's past deliverance from the house of bondage, when Jehovah loved him and called him, as His son, out of the land dominated by the Pharaohs.

Is there then contradiction here? Far otherwise. There is the most perfect agreement, which another passage at once manifests. In II Corinthians 3 we learn from verse 17, read in connection with the entire chapter, that the Lord is the Spirit of the Old Testament. He is everywhere presented to the anointed eye. Hence the apostle wrote by divine inspiration when he declared that Hosea's words prophetically foretold the coming up of God's Son out of Egypt. In wondrous grace He would, as it were, begin as His people began, in regard to His earthly pilgrimage. So, as a Babe whose life is sought by Herod, He is carried over the route taken by Jacob when driven by famine to Egypt; and from that land whence His people had been delivered when oppressed by Pharaoh, He later returns to Palestine. Thus would He be identified with them in their wanderings, that they might understand how the Holy Spirit spoke of Him when He said, "In all their affliction he was afflicted, and the angel of his presence saved them" (Isa. 63:9).

Called out of Egypt, He was ever the One in whom the Father found delight. In this how blessedly opposite to Israel! Redeemed by power from Egyptian tyranny, they went far from Him, though He called them in tenderest love. Turning away, they sacrificed unto Baalim, and worshiped images of man's design (v. 2).

Yet He had taught Ephraim to take his earliest steps, as it were; holding his arms and directing his way. But they soon, like an ungrateful child, forgot Him to whom they owed so much, and knew not that He had healed them. Tenderly He recalls those early days when He drew them with cords of a man and with bands of love, delivering them from the yoke, and providing all that they needed for their sustenance and enjoyment (vv. 3, 4) — what saint but will see in words so lovely the story of his own deliverance from sin and Satan, when first brought to the knowledge of Christ! Long enthralled in worse than Egyptian bondage, how unspeakably precious was the earliest revelation of His grace to our souls, when He drew us to Himself from our wickedness and waywardness by the bands of love; which were indeed the cords of a man—the Man Christ Jesus, who gave Himself a ransom for all! Let us challenge our hearts as to what return we have made to love so deep and tender. What is the Baal that has lured some of us so far from Him who once was everything to our hearts, when we took our first steps out into the wilderness with Him to whom we owed so much? Rest assured, fellow-believer, till every idol is destroyed, we shall never know again the freshness and joy of those early days, if we have allowed other lords to have dominion over us.

Once set free from Egypt, Israel, nationally, could never return there. But because of their sins, they were given into the hand of the Assyrian; as will, in a more awful manner, be the case in the last days, when the sword shall abide upon them, "because of their own counsels" (vv. 5, 6).

Such must be the bitter fruit of forgetting their God and taking their own foolish and sinful way. From the first they had been "bent to backsliding" from Him, though He had called them again and again to repentance. But they persisted in their folly till there was no remedy (v. 7).

Yet His yearning heart causes Him to cry, "How shall I give thee up ... mine heart is turned within me, my repentings are kindled together" (v. 8). He could not bear to make them as the cities of the nations upon whom His wrath had fallen without any mixture of mercy. Zeboiim and Admah (see Gen. 14:8) were two of the cities of the plain blotted out in the day when Sodom and Gomorrah fell beneath His judgment (Deut. 29:23). Of a similar doom Moses warned Israel if they failed to keep His holy law. Thus they were righteously under that awful sentence; but God, falling back upon His own sovereignty, declares, "I will not execute the fierceness of mine anger, I will not return to destroy Ephraim: for I am God, and not man; the Holy One in the midst of thee: and I will not enter into the city"—*i.e.*, to utterly consume it (v. 9).

It is most blessed to realize that God, who, once He has given His word in grace, will never repent, or permit that people to be cursed whom He has blessed (as He made known to Balaam), yet reserves to Himself the right to turn from the greatness of His wrath, however richly deserved, and manifest His loving-kindness to the people of His choice upon their repentance. Therefore, though He might righteously have utterly destroyed Ephraim, He preserved a remnant, in grace, who shall yet be to the praise of His glory in the land of their fathers; when "They shall walk after the LORD," in the day that "he shall roar like a lion," (v. 10) causing His once-blinded people to tremble at His word; when He shall "set his hand again the second time to recover the remnant of his people, which shall be left, from Assyria, and from Egypt, and from Pathros, and from Cush, and from Elam, and from Shinar, and from Hamath, and from the islands of the sea" (Isa. 11:11). At His call they will come, weeping because of their sin, yet rejoicing in His love; "as a bird out of Egypt, and as a dove out of the land of Assyria," to be placed "in their houses," never again to be removed, according to the word of Jehovah (v. 11).

This verse completes another distinct division of the prophecy, which extends from their first call out of Egypt to their restoration to the land and to God in the days of the millennial kingdom.

The last verse is properly the introduction to chapter 12, and brings in a new subject, which closes with the end of chapter 13. When Hosea prophesied, as frequently noted, the iniquity of Judah was not yet so manifest as that of the ten tribes whom Jeroboam had led astray from the very beginning, turning them away from Jehovah, and setting up the golden calves for their worship. They had been idolatrous from the first, and all their kings had followed in the steps of "Jeroboam the son of Nebat, which made Israel to sin." Therefore sentence was early pronounced on them because God had to say, "Ephraim compasseth me about with lies, and the house of Israel with deceit" (v. 12). There had never been any response to the many warnings and entreaties sent them by the Lord.

But with Judah it was far otherwise. Among them, decline was a matter of slow, and sometimes thwarted, progress. Hence we read, "But Judah yet ruleth with God, and is faithful with the saints" (v. 12, margin). Up to the time when Hosea prophesied, there was still a measure of devotion to Jehovah in Judah. Moreover, revival after revival followed the fervent calls to repentance uttered by the prophets; but it will be observed that as the years went on, they too became less and less responsive to the voice of God, until they lost all concern for His holiness.*

---

*Hypocrisy, therefore, developed especially in Judah—"This people honoureth me with their *lips*, but their *heart* is far from me" (Mark 7:6; Isa. 29:13). This is the danger where doctrine is right and outward form correct while the heart is away from God. Let every child of God beware of this. See Luke 12:1.—Ed.

8
Restoration and Blessing

The same yearning tenderness that led the rejected Messiah to weep over Jerusalem as He said, "If thou hadst known, even thou, at least in this thy day, the things which belong unto thy peace!" (Luke 19:42) is manifest throughout this final chapter of our prophet. It is one of the most touching yet faithful entreaties to be found in the Book of God, reminding us of the soul-stirring appeals uttered by the Holy Spirit through a later servant, Jeremiah. Not only does it give us the beseechings of Jehovah that His people heed His voice and return to Himself, but it sets forth clearly just how they should go about it, even putting into their lips the words which, if they came from their hearts, He would delight to hear. Abundant promises too are given of blessing to be poured out upon them when they should thus bow before Him in repentance and contrition of heart.

"O Israel, return unto the LORD thy God; for thou hast fallen by thine iniquity" (v. 1). How bitterly had they proven that "the way of transgressors is hard" (Prov. 13:15). "Righteousness," we are elsewhere told, "exalteth a nation: but sin is a reproach to any people" (Prov.

14:34). Had they followed in the paths of uprightness which their faithful, covenant-keeping God had marked out for them, theirs had been a very different history. But they refused to hearken, and turned away the shoulder. The result was failure and disaster from first to last. They had indeed fallen very low. Yet He, who had been so grievously sinned against, could lovingly entreat them still to return unto Him, who was their God from the land of Egypt.

Let us learn from their unhappy course both to avoid their sins and to know the exceeding grace of our God. The Church, as a testimony for an absent Lord, has failed as fully as Israel. But however dark the day, wherever a true heart turns back to God, judging itself for participation in the common sin of those so highly privileged, He who has been so grievously dishonored will still gladly receive such an one; yea, He waits but for open doors to come in and sup in communion, though the hour be late.

If the soul say, "But I have erred so seriously, I know not how to approach so holy a God after having dishonored Him to such an extent;" then He Himself will put a prayer into the lips of the returning one: thus assuring each seeking soul of His willingness to hear. "Take with you words, and turn to the LORD: say unto him, Take away all iniquity, and receive us graciously: so will we render the calves of our lips. Asshur shall not save us; we will not ride upon horses: neither will we say any more to the work of our hands, Ye are our gods: for in thee the fatherless findeth mercy" (vv. 2, 3).

This prayer, indited by God Himself, will repay the most careful consideration. Let us take up its clauses one by one, weighing each in the presence of the Lord. "Take away all iniquity, and receive us graciously," cries the repentant soul. Having long been defiled, till the conscience was almost calloused, the light of God has now shown things up as they really are. This produces an abhorrence of the waywardness so long tolerated as though it were a thing indifferent. Unconcern is succeeded by deep exercise. "Take away all iniquity" is the soul's longing. Sin becomes hateful the moment one gets into the presence of God. Then the need of grace is felt, and so the cry comes, "receive us graciously." What a mercy that it is to "the God of *all grace*" we are directed to come!

There can be no restoration so long as one sin is trifled with and remains unjudged; but the instant a full confession is made and all iniquity is honestly turned from, the Word assures us of instant forgiveness. "If we confess our sins, he is faithful and just to forgive us our sins, and to cleanse us from all unrighteousness" (I John 1:9). This is the principle that applies to a lost sinner seeking salvation, or an erring saint desiring restoration of soul. Sin judged is sin gone; and the soul may afresh enjoy the communion that has been interrupted from the moment evil was allowed upon the conscience. In the knowledge of this—a knowledge received, not by feelings, but resting on the testimony of Scripture—praise and worship once more spring up in the heart. "So will we render the calves of our lips."

Only when the life is right and the conscience pure from defilement can there be worship in spirit and in truth. Then the happy saint can without hindrance pour forth into the ear of God his grateful praises, and his worship, like incense, arise from the heart to which Christ is all. Israel shall enter into this, when, restored to their land after their disciplinary wanderings, they rejoice before Him who shall dwell in the midst of them, having first purged them with the spirit of burning from all that has hindered their full acknowledgment of His grace.

"Asshur shall not save us," is the cry of a people who

have learned to "Cease ye from man, whose breath is in his nostrils" (Isa. 2:22). We have seen throughout this book how in the hour of their distress they turned, not to God against whom they had revolted, but to Assyria, the proud northern power, who was destined to be their ruin. Thus they learned that "vain is the help of man." Therefore they will say in the day of Jehovah's might, "Asshur shall not deliver us;"* but in God alone will they find their Saviour.

Nor will they depend in that day upon their own armies, mounted like the cavalry of the nations. "We will not ride upon horses." It is noticeable throughout this history that their strength for warfare consisted not in imitating the manners and customs of the nations, but in reliance upon God in the spirit of praise. When Judah ("praise") led, they conquered, as they counted on the Lord alone for succor. When Jehoshaphat met the enemy, he put *singers*, not cavalrymen, in the van, and a great victory ensued. To this they shall return when humbled before God because of all their failure and sin. "A horse is a vain thing for safety," though it seem to add wonderfully to human prowess. But better far is it to lean upon the arm of Jehovah, and remember that the battle is His, not ours.

Idolatry had been their undoing in the past. But then they shall cry, "neither will we say any more to the work of our hands, Ye are our gods." Having learned the impotence of the "gods many and lords many" who have had dominion over them, the Lord alone shall be exalted in that day. It is a lovely picture of a soul who has proven that no power, seen or unseen, can avail for deliverance, but the strength of "the mighty God of Jacob." When

*It is usually God's way to cause the very thing in which His people have dishonored Him to become their chastisement—thus to deliver the heart from the idol it has sought after.—Ed.

everything is thus out in His presence, and no guile remains in their spirit, they can add with assurance, "For
in thee the fatherless findeth mercy." Israel had been
Jehovah's son, whom He had called out of Egypt. But
they had forgotten Him, and done despite to His Spirit
of grace. Therefore He had pronounced the Lo-ammi and
Lo-ruhamah sentences upon them, as we saw in the beginning of the prophecy. Thus, when they return, they
come in on the ground of pure grace and mercy. They
come as "the fatherless"; not to claim the rights of a
child, but to be the subjects of that lovingkindness which
is better than life. How suited to the lips of the Remnant
of the last days will be the words of this prayer!

The gracious response of the Lord immediately follows: "I will heal their backsliding, I will love them
freely: for mine anger is turned away from him" (v. 4). It
is as though His great heart of love had been full, nigh
to bursting, but their sins had kept Him from expressing
all that was there. Now every barrier is removed, and,
like an irresistible torrent, His kindness flows forth,
overleaping, or sweeping away, every obstruction that a
timid faith might yet raise. Loving them freely, He will
set them in paths of righteousness, healing their souls
and turning them from all their backslidings. Everything
of the dark past forgiven and gone, His wrath has van-
ished, and His grace knows no bounds.

No longer shall they be as a barren and desolate
heath, but like a watered garden, tended and kept by
Himself. "I will be as the dew unto Israel: he shall grow
as the lily, and cast forth his roots as Lebanon" (v. 5).
The dew ever, in Scripture, sets forth the refreshing in-
fluences of the Holy Spirit, ministering the truth in grace
to the soul. The manna in the wilderness fell on the
dew—type of Christ ministered in the power of the Holy
Ghost. Gideon's signs pictured in a marvelous way God's

varied dealings in this regard. At first the dew was on the fleece, while all the ground was dry. Again, the fleece was dry, but all the ground covered with dew. So had Israel been blessed with the Spirit's testimony, while the world lay in ignorance and idolatry. But Israel rejected Messiah at His first coming, and now the chosen nation is dry and desolate, while the Spirit of God is working among the Gentiles. In the Millennium He will be poured out on all flesh; then fleece and ground shall alike be refreshed with the dew. In Psalm 133 "the dew of Hermon" sets forth the same quickening and revivifying power as here in Hosea. God Himself will be as the dew unto His restored people, giving new life and freshness, that they may evermore rejoice in Him. Under His kindly nurture, they shall put on the beauty of the lily, with the strength of the cedar of Lebanon. No fading glory shall again be theirs, but a beauty that shall endure, and a strength that can never fail.

Then "His branches shall spread, and his beauty shall be as the olive tree, and his smell as Lebanon" (v. 6). Towering up to heaven like a mighty cedar, Israel's branches shall go out in majesty, and their fragrance shall be wafted in the air, that all may know that the Lord has taken them as His own. Nor is it only dignity and fragrance, but there shall be all the loveliness and fruitfulness of the olive tree—the oil tree, as the word might be rendered. This too speaks of the Holy Spirit, who will permeate the nation as the oil permeates the olive, making it a source of spiritual blessing to the whole earth.

"They that dwell under his shadow shall return; they shall revive as the corn, and grow as the vine: the scent thereof shall be as the wine of Lebanon" (v. 7). Figure after figure is pressed into service to tell the joy of the Lord in His people, and their beauty and preciousness in His eyes. Jacob shall not only be regathered, but others shall find blessing through him, according to the promise to the fathers. Many shall "dwell under his shadow," finding rest through the message committed to him. The corn and wine tell of strength and gladness. It shall no more be said, "Israel is an empty vine; he bringeth forth fruit unto himself." But, planted again in the land, the vine of the Lord shall flourish, and send forth its branches laden with choice clusters, to provide the wine of joy for the whole earth.

Then shall Ephraim say, "What have I to do any more with idols?" (v. 8). Dwelling in fellowship with God, and enjoying His matchless love and grace, the wretched follies of the past will be detested. The new affection will so possess the heart, that the vain idols at whose altars they once bowed will be hated and forgotten. In holy complacency the Lord looks down and says, "I have heard him, and observed him."* In joyous exultation, Israel answers, "I am like a green fir tree"—not temporary verdure; but, like an evergreen, they will be perennially fresh and lovely in His eyes. But all their goodness is from Himself; so He replies, "From me is thy fruit found." Apart from Him, all would be barrenness once more, even as Jesus said, "Without me, ye can do nothing." But, abiding in the uninterrupted enjoyment of His love, their fruit shall never fail nor their freshness ever depart.

This closes the prophecy; but pointedly the Lord presses upon every reader the importance of weighing all in His presence. "Who is wise, and he shall under-

---

*There is good ground here to question the proper construction of this dialogue. I have followed J. N. Darby's suggestion in "The Synopsis of the Books of the Bible." We might understand Israel as saying, "What have I to do any more with idols? I have heard Him, and observed Him! I am like a green fir tree." Then Jehovah's answer, "From Me is thy fruit found."

stand these things? prudent, and he shall know them? for the ways of the LORD are right, and the just shall walk in them: but the transgressors shall fall therein" (v. 9). *The ways of the Lord* has been the theme of Hosea. Happy shall we be if we are, through grace, numbered among the wise and prudent who know and understand, and the just who walk in them!

The Lord give efficacy to His Word for His name's sake! Amen.

Excerpt from
John

The Heart of the Gospel

9
The Heart of the Gospel

"For God so loved the world, that he gave his only begotten Son, that whosoever believeth in him should not perish, but have everlasting life. For God sent not his Son into the world to condemn the world; but that the world through him might be saved. He that believeth on him is not condemned: but he that believeth not is condemned already, because he hath not believed in the name of the only begotten Son of God. And this is the condemnation, that light is come into the world, and men loved darkness rather than light, because their deeds were evil. For every one that doeth evil hateth the light, neither cometh to the light, lest his deeds should be reproved. But he that doeth truth cometh to the light, that his deeds may be made manifest, that they are wrought in God" (John 3:16-21).

Martin Luther called this sixteenth verse the "Miniature Gospel," because there is a sense in which the whole story of the Bible is told out in it. "For God so loved the world, that he gave his only begotten Son, that whosoever believeth in him should not perish, but have everlasting life." The verse negates the idea that a great many persons seem to have; that God is represented in Scriptures as a stern, angry Judge waiting to destroy men because of their sins, but that Jesus Christ, in some way or other, has made it possible for God to come out in love to sinners; in other words, that Christ loved us enough to die for us and, having atoned for our sins, God can now love us and be merciful to us. But that is an utter perversion of the gospel. Jesus Christ did not die to enable God to love sinners, but "God so loved the world, that he gave his only begotten Son." This same precious truth is set forth in similar words in the fourth chapter of the First Epistle of John, "In this was manifested the love of God toward us, because that God sent his only begotten Son into the world, that we might live through him. Herein is love, not that we loved God, but that he loved us, and sent his Son to be the propitiation for our sins" (vv. 9, 10). So the coming to this world of our Lord Jesus Christ and His going to the cross, there to settle the sin question and thus meet every claim of the divine righteousness against the sinner, is the proof of the infinite love of God toward a world of guilty men. How we ought to thank and praise Him that He gave His Son for our redemption! "God commendeth his love toward us, in that, while we were yet sinners, Christ died for us." It could not be otherwise, because He is love. We are taught that in I John 4:8, 16. "God is love." That is His very nature. We can say that God is gracious, but we cannot say that God is grace. We can say that God is compassionate, but we cannot say that God is compassion. God is kind, but God is not kindness. But we can say, God is love. That is His nature, and love had to manifest itself, and although men had forfeited every claim that they might have upon God, still He loved us and sent His only Son to become the propitiation for our sins—"God so loved the world that He gave His only begotten Son, that whosoever believeth in Him should not perish, but have everlasting life."

Our Lord Jesus Christ is spoken of five times as the "only begotten" in the New Testament: twice in the first chapter of this Gospel. In verse 14 we read, "the Word was made flesh, and dwelt among us, (and we beheld his glory, the glory as of the only begotten of the Father,) full of grace and truth." Also in verse 18, "No man hath seen God at any time; the only begotten Son, which is in the bosom of the Father, he hath declared him." Then here is this sixteenth verse of the third chapter, "God so loved . . . that he gave his only begotten . . ." Again in verse 18, "he that believeth not is condemned already, because he hath not believed in the name of the only begotten Son of God." The only other place where this term is used is in I John 4:9, "God sent his only begotten Son into the world, that we might live through him." It is a singular fact, and shows how wonderfully Scripture is constructed, that that term is not only used five times in the New Testament, but He is also called the "first begotten" or "the first born" exactly five times in the same book.

Now "only begotten" refers to His eternal Sonship. The term, "the first begotten," tells what He became, in grace, as Man, for our redemption. When He came into the world God owned that blessed Man as His first begotten, saying, "Thou art my Son: this day have I begotten thee" (Ps. 2:7). The term "only begotten" does not carry in it any thought of generation, but that of uniqueness—Son by special relationship. The word is used in connection with Isaac. We read that Abraham "offered up his only begotten." Now Isaac was not his only son. Ishmael was born some years before Isaac, so in the sense of generation you would not speak of Isaac as the only begotten son. He is called the "only begotten" because he was born in a miraculous manner, when it seemed impossible that Abraham and Sarah could ever be the parents of a child. In the Spanish translation we read that "God so loved the world that he gave his unique Son"; that is, our Lord Jesus Christ is the Son of God in a sense that no one else can ever be the Son of God — His eternal Son — His unique Son. Oh, how dear to the heart of the Father! And when God gave Him, He not only became incarnate to bear hardship and weariness and thirst and hunger, but God gave Him up to the death of the cross that there He might be the propitiation for our sins. Could there be any greater manifestation of divine love than this?

You remember the story of the little girl in Martin Luther's day, when the first edition of the Bible came out. She had a terrible fear of God. God had been presented in such a way that it filled her heart with dread when she thought of Him. She brooded over the awfulness of the character of God and of some day having to meet this angry Judge. But one day she came running to her mother, holding a scrap of paper in her hand. She cried out, "Mother! mother! I am not afraid of God any more." Her mother said, "Why are you not?" "Why, look, mother," she said, "this bit of paper I found in the print shop, and it is torn out of the Bible." It was so torn as to be almost illegible except about two lines. On the one line it said, "God so loved," and on the other line it said, "that he gave." "See, mother," she said, "that makes it all right." Her mother read it and said, "God so loved that he gave." "But," she said, "it does not say what he gave." "Oh, mother," exclaimed the child, "if He loved us enough to give anything, it is all right." Then the mother said, "But, let me tell you what He gave." She read, "God so loved the world, that he gave his only begotten Son, that whosoever believeth in him should not perish, but have everlasting life." Then she told how we can have peace and eternal life through trusting Him.

Am I speaking to anyone today who dreads the thought of meeting God? Do you think of your sins and say with David of old, "I remembered God and was troubled"? Let me call your attention to this word: The love of God has been manifest in Christ. If you will but come as a needy sinner He will wash your sins away. "But," you say, "how can I be sure that it is for me? I can understand that God could love some people. I can understand how He can invite certain ones to trust Him. Their lives have been so much better than mine, but I cannot believe that this salvation is for me." Well, what else can you make from that word, "whosoever"? "God so loved ... that He gave ... that whosoever believeth in him should not perish, but have everlasting life." He could not find another more all-embracing word than that. It takes you in. It takes me in. You have many another "whosoever" in the Bible. There is a "whosoever" of judgment: "whosoever was not found written in the book of life was cast into the lake of fire" (Rev. 20:15). "Whosoever" there includes all who did not come to God while He waited, in grace, to save. If they had recognized that they were included in the "Whosoever" of John 3:16, they would not be found in that of Revelation 20:15.

Somebody wrote me the other day and said, "A man has come to our community who is preaching a limited atonement. He says it is a wonderful truth that has been only recently revealed to him." Well, I could only write back that the term "limited atonement" has an uncanny sound to me. I do not read anything like that in my Bible. I read that "He tasted death for every man." I read that "He is the propitiation for our sins, and not for our sins only, but for the whole world." I read that "All we like sheep have gone astray; we have turned every one to his own way; and the LORD hath laid on him the iniquity of us all." And here I read that "Whosoever believeth in him should not perish, but have everlasting life." I say to you, as I said to the writer of that letter, that there is enough value in the atoning work of the Lord Jesus Christ to save every member of the human race, if they would but repent and turn to God; and then if they were all saved, there still remains value enough to save the members of a million worlds like this, if they are lost in sin and needing a Saviour. Yes, the sacrifice of Christ is an infinite sacrifice. Do not let the enemy of your soul tell you there is no hope for you. Do not let him tell you you have sinned away your day of grace; that you have gone so far that God is no longer merciful. There is life abundant for you if you will but look up into the face of the One who died on Calvary's cross and trust Him for yourself. Let me repeat it again, "Whosoever believeth in him should not perish, but have everlasting life."

"Whosoever believeth." What is it to believe? It is to trust in Him; to confide in Him; to commit yourself and your affairs to Him. He is saying to you, poor needy sinner, "You cannot save yourself. All your efforts to redeem yourself can only end in failure, but I have given My Son to die for you. Trust in Him. Confide in Him!" "Whosoever believeth in him should not perish."

A lady was reading her Greek Testament one day. She was studying the Greek language and she liked to read in the Greek Testament. She had no assurance of salvation. While pondering over these words, "whosoever believeth," she said to herself as she looked at the Greek word for *believeth*, "I saw this a few verses back." She went back in the chapter, and then back into the last verse of chapter two, and she read, "Many believed in His name when they saw the miracles which He did. But Jesus did not commit Himself unto them, because He knew all men." "Oh," she said, "there it is!" "Jesus did not commit Himself unto them," and she stopped and thought a moment, and light from heaven flashed into her soul. She saw that to believe in Jesus was to commit herself unto Jesus. Have you done that? Have you said,

"Jesus, I will trust Thee, trust Thee with my soul,
Weary, worn and helpless, Thou canst make me whole.
There is none in heaven, or on earth like Thee;
Thou hast died for sinners; therefore, Lord, for me."

Now, "whosoever believeth in him should not perish." As you turn the pages of Holy Scripture you get a marked picture of those who refused this grace. To perish means to go out into the darkness; to be forever under judgment; to exist in awful torment. He wants to save you from that. "Whosoever believeth in him should not perish, but have everlasting life."

"Have," that suggests present possession. He does not say, "*hope* to have everlasting life." You will have everlasting life right here and now when you believe in Jesus, when you trust Him. Somebody pondered about this one day and then he looked up and said, "God loved — God gave — I believe — and I have — everlasting life." Everlasting life, remember, is far more than life throughout eternity. It is far more than endless existence. It is the very life of God communicated to the soul in order that we may enjoy fellowship with Him. "This is life eternal, that they might know thee, the only true God, and Jesus Christ, whom thou hast sent."

In verse 17, as though to encourage the guiltiest to

come to Him, He says, "For God sent not his Son into the world to condemn the world; but that the world through him might be saved."

I remember, years ago, a dear old man behind the counter in a big department store in Los Angeles, where I worked as a lad. The old man was very kind to me. He saw that I was very green and knew not what was expected of me. He took me under his wing and cared for me. I soon got interested in finding out whether he was saved or not. My dear mother was never with anybody very long before she asked them the question, "Are you saved? Are you born again?" I became so used to hearing her ask that question that I thought I ought to ask it of people too. I went to him one day and said, "Mr. Walsh, are you saved?" He looked at me and said, "My dear boy, no one will ever know that until the day of judgment." "Oh," I replied, "there must be some mistake; my mother knows she is saved." "Well, she has made a mistake," he said; "for no one can know that." "But the Bible says, 'He that believeth on him . . . hath everlasting life.' " "Oh, well," he said, "we can't be sure down here unless we become great saints; but we must just do the best we can and pray to the Lord and the blessed Virgin and the saints to help, and hope that in the day of judgment it may turn out well and we will be saved." "But," I said, "why do you pray to the blessed Virgin? Why not go direct to Jesus?" "My dear boy, the Lord is so great and mighty and holy that it is not befitting that a poor sinner such as I should go to Him, and there is no other who has such influence as His mother." I did not know how to answer him then. But as I studied my Bible through the years, I could see what the answer was. Jesus unapproachable! Jesus hard to be contacted! Why, it was said of Him, "This man receiveth sinners," and though high in heavenly glory, He still says to sinners, "Come unto me all ye that labor and are heavy laden." Yes, you can go directly to Him and when you trust Him He gives you eternal life. He did not come to condemn the world. He came with a heart of love to win poor sinners to Himself.

And then the eighteenth verse is so plain and simple. Oh, if you are an anxious soul and seeking light, remember that these are the very words of the living God, "He that believeth on him is not condemned: but he that believeth not is condemned already, because he hath not believed in the name of the only begotten Son of God." Now, do you see this? There are just two classes of people in that verse. All men in the world who have heard the message are divided into these two classes. What are they? First, "He that believeth." There are those who believe in Jesus. They stand by themselves. Now the other class, "he that believeth not." Every person who has ever heard of Jesus is in one of those two classes. You are either among those who believe in Jesus or among those who do not believe. It is not a question of believing *about* Him; it is a question of believing *in* Him. It is not holding mental conceptions about Him, mere facts of history; but it is trusting Him, committing yourself to Him. Those who trust Him and those who do not trust Him—in which of the two groups do you find yourself? "He that believeth in him": are you there? "He that believeth not": are you there? Oh, if you are, you should be in a hurry to get out of that group into the other, and you pass out of the one and into the other by trusting in Jesus.

Are you in the first group? "He that believeth in him is not condemned." Do you believe that? Jesus said that. "He that believeth in him is not condemned."

I was in Kilmarnock three years ago and gave an address one night in the Grant Hall, and a number of people had come into the inquiry room and I went in afterwards to see how they were getting along. A minister called me over and said, "Will you have a word with this lad?" I sat down beside him and said, "What is the trouble?" He looked up and said, "I canna see it. I canna see it. I am so burdened, and canna find deliverance." I said, "Have you been brought up in a Christian home?" He told me he had. "Do you know the way of salvation?" He answered, "Well, in a way, I do; but I canna see it." I said, "Let me show you something." First I prayed with him and asked God, by the Holy Spirit, to open his heart. Then I pointed him to this verse and said, "Do you see those two classes of people? What is the first class? What is the second class? He answered clearly. "Now," I said, "which class are you in?" Then he looked at me and said, "Why, I am in the first class. I do believe in Him, but it is all dark. I canna see." "Now look again," said I. "What does it say about the first class?" He did look again and I could see the cloud lift, and he turned to me and exclaimed, "Man, I see it! I am not condemned." I asked, "How do you know?" He replied, "God said so." The minister said, "Well, lad, are you now willing to go home and tell your parents? Tomorrow when you go to work, will you be willing to tell your mates?" "Oh," he said, "I can hardly wait to get there."

Now, suppose you are in the other group. Listen, "He that believeth not is condemned already." You do not need to wait till the day of judgment to find that out. Condemned! Why? Because you have been dishonest? Because you have lied? Because you have been unclean and unholy? Is it that? That is not what it says *here*. What does it say? "He that *believeth not* is condemned already because he hath not believed in the name of the only begotten Son of God." That is the condemnation.

All those sins you have been guilty of, Christ took into account when He died. "He was wounded for our transgressions, he was bruised for our iniquities: the chastisement of our peace was upon him; and with his stripes we are healed" (Isa. 53:5). So, if you are condemned, it is not simply because of the many sins you have committed through your lifetime. It is because of spurning the revelation of the Saviour that God has provided. If you turn away from God and continue rejecting Jesus, you are committing the worst sin there is. He came, a light, into the world to lighten the darkness. If you turn away from Him, you are responsible for the darkness in which you will live and die.

"And this is the condemnation, that light is come into the world, and men loved darkness rather than light, because their deeds were evil." Is it not strange that men would rather continue in darkness than turn to Him, who is the light of life, and find deliverance? "For every one that doeth evil hateth the light, neither cometh to the light, lest his deeds should be reproved. But he that doeth truth [*i.e.*, he that is absolutely honest with God] cometh to the light, that his deeds may be made manifest, that they are wrought in God." Are you going to turn away from the light today or are you coming into the light? Will you trust the blessed One who is the light of the world, and thus rejoice in the salvation which He so freely offers you?

James and Peter

The New Life Contrasted with the Old
Increasing Apostasy and the Call to
Righteousness (partial)

10
The New Life Contrasted with the Old

Conversion to God involves an inward and an outward change. When born again one receives a new nature with new desires and new ambitions. The whole behavior is changed from that of a selfish worldling to a devoted follower of the Lord Jesus Christ. The great importance of this is emphasized in the opening verses of this chapter.

"Forasmuch then as Christ hath suffered for us in the flesh, arm yourselves likewise with the same mind: for he that hath suffered in the flesh hath ceased from sin; That he no longer should live the rest of his time in the flesh to the lusts of men, but to the will of God. For the time past of our life may suffice us to have wrought the will of the Gentiles, when we walked in lasciviousness, lusts, excess of wine, revellings, banquetings, and abominable idolatries: Wherein they think it strange that ye run not with them to the same excess of riot, speaking evil of you: Who shall give account to him that is ready to judge the quick and the dead. For this cause was the gospel preached also to them that are dead, that they might be judged according to men in the flesh, but live according to God in the spirit. But the end of all things is at hand; be ye therefore sober, and watch unto prayer" (I Peter 4:1-7).

With Christ Himself as our example of patience in suffering how can we, who owe all to Him, do otherwise than arm ourselves with the same mind and so endure as beholding Him by faith? Many times God uses suffering to keep us from going into that which would dishonor Him. And when exposed to severe temptation it is as we suffer in the flesh that we are kept from sin. In this we may see the difference between our Lord's temptations and those which we have to face. He was tempted in all points like as we, apart from sin. He did not have a sinful nature as we do. He was from His birth the Holy One. He could say, "The prince of this world cometh and hath nothing in me." With us it is otherwise. When Satan attacks from without there is an enemy within, "sin, the flesh," that responds to his appeal, and it is only as we reckon ourselves dead indeed unto sin but alive unto God that we are enabled to mortify the deeds of the body. This means suffering, often of a very severe character. But, we are told, Jesus "suffered being tempted" (Heb. 2:18). So infinitely pure and holy was He that it caused Him intense suffering even to be exposed to Satan's solicitations. He overcame by the Word of God, and the devil left Him for a season, to return in the hour of His agony as He was bearing our sins upon the cross.

Let us therefore resist every temptation to gratify the flesh, cost what it may, for it is our new responsibility to live no longer in the flesh according to carnal desires, but in the Spirit to the glory of God. A careful consideration of Galatians 5 will help to make clear what Peter here presents to us as to our responsibility to refrain from ways that once characterized us. In their unsaved

days these whom he addresses wrought the will of the
Gentiles when they fellowshipped with the ungodly in
lasciviousness, lusts, excess of wine, revellings, banquetings, and the abominations connected with idolatry. Although after the flesh, the Jews sought to curry favor
with their pagan Gentile neighbors by participation in
these evil things, even as Israel of old failed so grievously
at Baal-Peor (Num. 25:1-3). Since their conversion to
God all this was changed. Their former companions could
not understand why they so suddenly and completely
turned from lives of self-indulgence to what seemed to
them great abstemiousness and austerity. They who applauded them before, now spoke evil of them. But they
were to live as those who should give account not to
men, but to Him who is about to judge the living and
the dead when He returns in power. In that day those
who despised them for their holy lives would answer to
God too. "For this cause was the gospel preached also
to them that are dead, that they might be judged according to men in the flesh, but live according to God
in the spirit." Those who had preceded them in the path
of faith were obliged to contend with similar conditions.
The good news preached to them who, though now dead,
once had to face the ridicule and even persecution of
wicked men who had no understanding of spiritual things,
was revealed to them that even while living as men in
this scene and judged by their fellows as fools and fa-
natics, they might actually live unto God in spirit. There
is no thought or suggestion here of the gospel being
carried to men after death as Romanists, Mormons, and
others, would have us believe.

Verse 7 — The Christian is ever to keep the end in
view. He is to live not for the passing moment, but as
one who knows that the end of all things — that is, all
things of this present order, is at hand. It will be ushered

in at the Lord's return; therefore, the importance of sobriety and watchfulness unto prayer.

Suffering as a Christian

The name "Christian" is not found very often in the New Testament, but is the distinctive title of those who belong to Christ. We read of it in Acts 11:26 where it was conferred upon the Gentile believers at Antioch by divine authority; for the word "called" there literally means "oracularly called," and therefore it was not the Antiochians alone who bestowed this name upon the believers, but God Himself who so designated them. That it has become their well-known appellation is evident from Acts 26:28, where we read that King Agrippa exclaimed, "Almost thou persuadest me to be a Christian." When Peter wrote this letter some years later he uses it as the commonly recognized name of the pilgrim company, and he tells us that it is praiseworthy to suffer as a Christian.

"Beloved, think it not strange concerning the fiery trial which is to try you, as though some strange thing happened unto you: But rejoice, inasmuch as ye are partakers of Christ's sufferings; that, when his glory shall be revealed, ye may be glad also with exceeding joy. If ye be reproached for the name of Christ, happy are ye; for the spirit of glory and of God resteth upon you: on their part he is evil spoken of, but on your part he is glorified. But let none of you suffer as a murderer, or as a thief, or as an evildoer, or as a busybody in other men's matters. Yet if any man suffer as a Christian, let him not be ashamed; but let him glorify God on this behalf. For the time is come that judgment must begin at the house of God: and if it first begin at us, what shall the end be of them that obey not the gospel of God? And if the righteous scarcely be saved, where shall the ungodly and the sinner appear? Wherefore let them that suffer according to the will of God commit the keeping of their souls to him in well doing, as unto a faithful Creator" (4:12-19).

In verse 12 he writes of "the fiery trial which is to try you." Primarily, the reference was to the great suffering that the Jews—whether Christian or not—were about to undergo in connection with the fulfilment of our Lord's prophecy concerning Jerusalem's destruction, shortly to take place (Luke 21:20-24). But it also has reference to the horrors of the Roman persecutions, which were to continue for two terrible centuries. The words are applicable to every time of trial and persecution.

Verse 13—"partakers of Christ's sufferings." The believer suffers in fellowship with his Lord. Our Lord has told us to expect this (John 15:18-21). We cannot be partakers of His atoning sufferings. They stand alone: none but He could endure the penalty for our sins and so make propitiation, in order that we might be forgiven. But we share His sufferings for righteousness' sake.

Verse 14—"reproached for the name of Christ." No one can be true to Christ and loved by the world-system, for everything that Jesus taught condemns the present order and leads ungodly men to hate Him and His people. But he who suffers for Christ's sake now is assured of glory hereafter, which will fully answer to the shame now endured. "On their part he is evil spoken of, but on your part he is glorified." The reproach of the world should not deter the Christian. He need not expect the approval of those who reject and misunderstand his Saviour. It is his responsibility so to live as to give the lie to the false reports of the ungodly and so to glorify the One whose name they spurn.

Verse 15—No believer should ever suffer as "a busybody in other men's matters." Notice the company in

which the busybody is placed. He is linked with mur-
derers, thieves, and evildoers of every description, and
that for a very good reason; for the busybody steals men's
reputations, seeks to assassinate their good names, and
by his calumniations works all manner of evil. The follower of Christ is called upon to be careful never to
misbehave so as to deserve the ill-will of the wicked. He
is not to be dishonest or corrupt in life, nor to be given
to gossipy interference in other people's affairs. Thus by
a holy and righteous life, he will adorn the gospel of
Christ (Phil. 1:27, 28).

Verse 16 — "if any man suffer as a Christian, let him
not be ashamed." None needs to be ashamed to suffer
because of his faithfulness to the hallowed name he bears.
The disciples, as we have noticed already, were called
Christians first at Antioch (Acts 11:26), and this name
has clung to them ever since. It signifies their union with
Christ, and therefore is a name in which to glory, however the world may despise it! Let us therefore never be
ashamed of this name and all that it implies, but be
prepared to suffer because of it, knowing that we may
thus glorify the God who has drawn us to Himself and
saves us through His blessed Son, who bore our sins in
His own body on the tree (I Peter 2:24).

Verse 17 — "judgment must begin at the house of God."
Our Father-God does not pass over the failures of His
people, but disciplines them in order that they may be
careful to walk in obedience to His Word. If He is thus
particular in chastening His own, how solemn will be
the judgment of "them that obey not the gospel," but
persist to the end in rejecting the Saviour He has provided!

Verse 18 — "if the righteous scarcely be saved," that
is, if the righteous have to endure chastening at the hand
of God and persecution at the hand of the world, what
will it mean for unsaved and impenitent men to answer

before the judgment-throne for their persistence in refusing His grace?

Verse 19 — "commit the keeping of their souls ... in well doing, as unto a faithful Creator." However hard the way and however perplexing their experiences, the suffering Christian may look up to God in confidence, knowing he can rely upon the divine love and faithfulness, and assured that all will work out for blessing at last.

Throughout the entire Christian era, which is that of the dispensation of the grace of God (Eph. 3:2), believers in Christ are called out from the world and are responsible to live for the glory of Him who has saved them. But though separated from the surrounding evil, they are not to shut themselves up as in a monastery or convent in order to be protected from defilement, but are to go forth as God's messengers into that very world from which they have been delivered, preaching to all men everywhere the gospel, which is God's offer of salvation through the finished work of His beloved Son. Whatever suffering or affliction this entails is to be borne cheerfully for His sake, knowing that He will reward abundantly for all endured, when He returns in glory. His Church is to be in the world, but not of it, witnessing rather against its evil, and offering pardon through the cross. Tertullian declared that the blood of the martyrs is the seed of the Church. This has been demonstrated over and over again. Persecution can never destroy the Church of God. The more it is called to suffer for Christ, the stronger it becomes. It is internal strife and carelessness in life that endangers it.

11
Increasing Apostasy and the Call to Righteousness

False doctrines had begun already to make serious inroads into the churches scattered throughout the world, as Paul's later letters give evidence, and as that of Jude also bears witness. Peter had this in mind when he gave his final message to the saints; but he foresaw even greater apostasy in days to come, and so gave an inspired word of warning in order that the believers might not be carried away by the personality and persuasiveness of false teachers masquerading as servants of Christ.

The close connection between this chapter and the Epistle of Jude has been noted often, and has given rise in some quarters to the idea that one is but a mutilated copy of the other. What we need to keep in mind is that the Holy Spirit Himself inspired both of these writers to portray conditions which the Church of God would have to face in years to come. While they cover the same ground to some extent, there is one very striking difference between them: Peter emphasizes the spread of unscriptural theories; whereas Jude dwells more particularly upon the effects of these, turning the grace of God into

114

lasciviousness; thus they give a twofold warning designed to save the elect of God from being misled. When once we realize that the Holy Spirit Himself is the Author of all Scripture we will not be surprised to find that He speaks in similar terms through different servants; in fact, we should naturally expect this. "The testimony of two men is true," we are told; and by this double testimony God emphasizes those things which we need to keep in mind.

Lessons from the Past for the Present Age

In verses 1 to 3 Peter turns our minds back to conditions that prevailed in former days which have important lessons for us. Let us look at this passage with particular care.

> "But there were false prophets also among the people, even as there shall be false teachers among you, who privily shall bring in damnable heresies, even denying the Lord that bought them, and bring upon themselves swift destruction. And many shall follow their pernicious ways; by reason of whom the way of truth shall be evil spoken of." And through covetousness shall they with feigned words make merchandise of you: whose judgment now of a long time lingereth not, and their damnation slumbereth not" (II Peter 2:1-3).

After God brought Israel out of Egypt false prophets rose up from time to time to controvert the truth which He revealed through His specially anointed servants, from the days when Korah, Dathan, and Abiram opposed Moses right on down to the period immediately preceding the captivity of Israel and Judah under Assyria and Babylon respectively. God's true servants were opposed by these false prophets who sought to foist their own dreams upon the people instead of the truth as declared by those who were divinely enlightened. Similar conditions had begun already to prevail in Christian circles even in apostolic times, and God foresaw that false teachers would rise up throughout all the centuries prior to the coming again of our Lord Jesus Christ. These false teachers come in under cover. They bring in heresies privately or secretly. It is never customary for teachers of error to declare and oppose the truth openly in the beginning. As a rule they work in an underhanded way, seeking to gain the confidence of God's people before they make known their real views. Such false teachers often hide their doctrinal peculiarities by using orthodox terms to which, however, they attach an altogether different meaning than that which is ordinarily accepted. Once having wormed their way into the confidence of the people of God they go to the limit, even denying the Lord who bought them, and so exposing themselves to the judgment of God. If they alone were thus dealt with it would be comparatively a small thing, but the sad result of their unscriptural ministry is that the weak and uninstructed readily follow the pernicious ways of these misleading representatives of Satan, and because of this the way of truth—that is, "the faith which was once delivered unto the saints"—is derided and evil spoken of.

We could instance many such cases today in various circles where the greatest and most precious things of God are spurned and held up to ridicule by those who have imbibed false views through giving heed to these heretical teachers. Heresy is like leaven. As the Apostle Paul tells us when combating Jewish legality which was spreading among the Galatians, "A little leaven leaveneth the whole lump" (Gal. 5:9). Leaven is corruption, and its nature is to corrupt all with which it comes in contact. So it is with false doctrine.

Back of every system of error is the sin of covetousness. Men seek to draw away disciples after themselves in order that they may make gain of them, and so as Peter here explains, "Through covetousness shall they with feigned words make merchandise of you." If it were not for the money question one wonders how long many systems of error would survive. Alas, that any should be so sordid as to seek to enrich themselves through the credulity of the souls whom they lead astray. The judgment of such is like a Damocles sword hanging over their heads, and though it seems to slumber for the moment it will not be long before it falls with terrible effect upon all such blind leaders of the blind.

Characteristics of Apostate Teachers

In II Peter 2:11-17 we have further evidence of the true nature of these apostates.

> "Whereas angels, which are greater in power and might, bring not railing accusation against them before the Lord. But these, as natural brute beasts, made to be taken and destroyed, speak evil of the things that they understand not; and shall utterly perish in their own corruption; And shall receive the reward of unrighteousness, as they that count it pleasure to riot in the day time. Spots they are and blemishes, sporting themselves with their own deceivings while they feast with you; Having eyes full of adultery, and that cannot cease from sin; beguiling unstable souls: an heart they have exercised with covetous practices; cursed children: Which have forsaken the right way, and are gone astray, following the way of Balaam the son of Bosor, who loved the wages of unrighteousness; But was rebuked for his iniquity: the dumb ass speaking with man's voice forbad the madness of the prophet. These are wells without water, clouds that are carried with a tempest; to whom the mist of darkness is reserved for ever."

While these ungodly men vaunt themselves against all authority, human, angelic, or divine, the elect angels — those who have been preserved by God from falling into sin, who are greater far in power and might than men here on the earth — do not presume to bring railing accusations even against those of their own order who have apostatized from God. Jude tells us that Michael the archangel did not bring against Satan a railing accusation but simply said, "The Lord rebuke thee." But these apostate leaders behave like natural brute beasts who are made to be taken and destroyed. These brutes, not possessing intelligence, act in accordance with their own vicious appetites and are imitated by the false teachers against whom Peter warns, who rail against things which God has made known in His Word but which they do not understand. In refusing the truth they, of necessity, will be left to perish in their own corruption, and in due time will be rewarded according to the unrighteousness of their lives. They have lived as though their greatest object was to satisfy the desires of their own hearts. They have counted it a pleasure to riot in the daytime: the night will find them utterly unprepared for the judgment which they have so richly deserved.

As these teachers of error mingle among the people of God they are spots and blemishes, marring and disturbing the fellowship of the saints, giving themselves over to self-indulgence as they feast with Christians as though they belonged to the family of God. Because there is no power in error to subdue nature's sinful lusts they are described as having eyes full of adultery; they cannot cease from sin. It is only the might of the Holy Spirit which can subdue and hold in check the lusts of the flesh. False doctrines never do this. While beguiling or leading astray unstable souls — that is, those who are not well-grounded in the truth of God, they prove themselves to be an accursed generation whose hearts are exercised not unto godliness but with covetous practices.

Verse 15 tells us that having forsaken the right way they have gone astray, following the way of Balaam, the son of Bosor, who loved the wages of unrighteousness. While pretending to be subject to the Lord, Balaam craved the riches which Balak offered him if he could curse Israel for him. As Balaam hastened on his way, lured by the desire of gain, even the beast on which he rode rebuked him, as it beheld an angel of God in the way who sought to turn back the covetous prophet from his path. Men may ridicule and sneer at the idea of an ass speaking with a man's voice, but he who knows the Lord will remember that with God all things are possible.

While the propagators of unholy and unscriptural theories profess to have just the message that men need, they actually have nothing that can give victory over sin or relief to a troubled conscience. They are like wells without water which only disappoint the thirsty who go to them, or like clouds that look as though they might soon pour down refreshing showers but are carried away by gales of wind, and so the land is left as dry and arid as ever. The doom of these misleading teachers is sure. The mist of darkness is to be their portion forever. The sad thing is that even among professing Christians so many are ready to listen to these pretentious vendors of false systems only to be destroyed at last when they find that they are left without anything upon which the heart and conscience can rest for eternity.

Turning Away from the Truth to the False Philosophies of the World

"For when they speak great swelling words of vanity, they allure through the lusts of the flesh, through much wantonness, those that were clean escaped from them who live in error. While they promise them liberty, they themselves are the servants of corruption: for of whom a man is overcome, of the same is he brought in bondage. For if after they have escaped the pollutions of the world through the knowledge of the Lord and Saviour Jesus Christ, they are again entangled therein, and overcome, the latter end is worse with them than the beginning. For it had been better for them not to have known the way of righteousness, than, after they have known it, to turn from the holy commandment delivered unto them. But it is happened unto them according to the true proverb, The dog is turned to his own vomit again; and the sow that was washed to her wallowing in the mire" (2:18-22).

It is one thing to accept Christianity as a system; it is quite another to know Christ as Saviour and Lord. Of all who are truly born again it can be said that "greater is he that is in you, than he that is in the world" (I John 4:4). These are kept from error as they go on in dependence upon the Word of God as it is opened up to them by the Holy Spirit. But those who have merely taken up with a system of doctrines, however sound, are always in danger of giving them up for some other system and so becoming apostates, ensnared by the vain-glorious language of false teachers who allure through the lusts of the flesh by presenting doctrines that appeal to hearts already turned wanton. Those who at one time had seemingly been completely delivered from sin and its folly are easily misled, and made to think that they are taking up with something superior to that which they already possess. But while these teachers promise their dupes liberty they themselves are slaves of corruption, because they know nothing of the liberty of grace, but rather are given to license instead. Overcome by sin they are brought into bondage.

Verses 20 and 21 have been taken by some as teaching that after people have been truly born again they are in danger of ceasing to be children of God and becoming once more the seed of Satan. It is well to observe that the Spirit of God is not contemplating reality here but simply profession. He speaks of those who have escaped the pollutions of the world through the knowledge of the Lord and Saviour Jesus Christ; that is, having accepted the doctrines of Christianity they have professedly given up the world, its sins and its folly, but there has never been a new nature imparted. They have not been born of God. Consequently, there is always the desire to gratify the lusts of the flesh, and when they come in contact with these false teachings they are easily entangled therewith and overcome, and so their latter end is worse with them than the beginning: that is, having given up the profession of Christianity and taken up with some false and unholy system of teaching they throw off all restraint as to their lusts and live even more vilely than they did before they made a profession of conversion. Of these Peter says, "it had been better for them not to have known the way of righteousness, than, after they have known it, to turn from the holy commandment delivered unto them." Anyone who becomes acquainted with the teachings of Christianity knows the way of righteousness. Men may give adherence to that way for the time being who do not actually know Christ for themselves. Of those who have thus apostatized we read, "it is happened unto them according to the true proverb, The dog is turned to his own vomit again; and the sow that was washed to her wallowing in the mire." Charles H. Spurgeon well said on one occasion, "If that dog or that sow had been born again and had received the nature of a sheep it never would have gone back to the filth here depicted." The dog is used as a symbol of false teachers on more than one occasion in Scripture. The sow is the natural man who may be cleansed outwardly but still loves the hog-wallow, and as soon as restraint is off he will go back to the filth in which he once lived.

Charge That to My Account

12

Charge That to My Account

"If thou count me therefore a partner,
receive him as myself. If he hath
wronged thee, or oweth thee ought,
put that on mine account; I Paul have
written it with mine own hand, I will
repay it; albeit I do not say to thee
how thou owest unto me even thine
own self besides" (Philem. 17-19).

Someone has said that this Epistle to Philemon
is the finest specimen of early private Christian correspondence extant. We should expect this, since it was
given by divine inspiration. And yet it all has to do with
a thieving runaway slave named Onesimus, who was about
to return to his former master.

The history behind the letter, which is deduced from
a careful study of the Epistle itself, seems to be this: In
the city of Colosse dwelt a wealthy Christian man by the
name of Philemon, possibly the head of a large house-
hold, and like many in that day, he had a number of

slaves or bondsmen. Christianity did not immediately overturn the evil custom of slavery, although eventually it was the means of practically driving it out of the whole civilized world. It began by regulating the relation of master and slave, thus bringing untold blessing to those in bondage.

This man Philemon evidently was converted through the ministry of the apostle Paul. Where they met, we are not told; certainly not in the city of Colosse, because in writing the letter to the Colossians, Paul makes it clear that he had never seen the faces of those who formed the Colossian church. You will recall that he labored at Ephesus for a long period. The fame of his preaching and teaching was spread abroad, and we read that "all in Asia heard the word." Among those who thus heard the Gospel message may have been this man Philemon of Colosse, and so he was brought to know Christ.

Some years had gone by, and this slave, Onesimus, had run away. Evidently before going, he had robbed his master. With his ill-gotten gains he had fled to Rome. How he reached there we do not know, but I have no doubt that upon his arrival he had his fling, and enjoyed to the full that which had belonged to his master. He did not take God into account, but nevertheless God's eye was upon him when he left his home, and it followed him along the journey from Colosse to Rome. When he reached that great metropolis, he was evidently brought into contact with the very man through whom his master, Philemon, had been converted. Possibly Onesimus was arrested because of some further rascality, and in that way came in contact with Paul in prison, or he may have visited him voluntarily. At any rate God, who knows just how to bring the needy sinner and the messenger of the Cross together, saw to it that Onesimus and Paul met face to face.

Sam Hadley Finds Jim

Some years ago there happened a wonderful illustration of this very thing: the divine ability to bring the needy sinner and the messenger of Christ together.

When Sam Hadley was in California, just shortly before he died, Dr. J. Wilbur Chapman, that princely man of God, arranged a midnight meeting, using the largest theatre in the city of Oakland, in order to get the message of Hadley before the very people who needed it most. On that night a great procession, maybe one thousand people, from all the different churches, led by the Salvation Army band, wended their way through the main streets of the city. Beginning at 10:30, they marched for one-half hour, and then came to the Metropolitan Theatre. In a moment or two it was packed from floor to gallery.

I happened to be sitting in the first balcony, looking right down upon the stage. I noticed that every seat on the stage was filled with Christian workers, but when Sam Hadley stepped forward to deliver the stirring message of the evening, his seat was left vacant. Just as he began to speak, I saw a man who had come in at the rear of the stage, slip around from behind the back curtain, and stand at one of the wings with his hand up to his ear, listening to the address. Evidently he did not hear very well. In a moment or two he moved to another wing, and then on to another one. Finally he came forward to one side of the front part of the stage and stood there listening, but still he could not hear very well. Upon noticing him, Dr. Chapman immediately got up, greeted the poor fellow, brought him to the front, and put him in the very chair which Sam Hadley had occupied. There he listened entranced to the story of Hadley's redemption.

When the speaker had finished, Dr. Chapman arose to

close the meeting, and Hadley took Chapman's chair next to this man. Turning to the man he shook hands with him, and they chatted together. When Dr. Chapman was about ready to ask the people to rise and receive the benediction, Hadley suddenly sprang to his feet, and said, "Just a moment, my friends. Before we close, Dr. Chapman, may I say something? When I was on my way from New York to Oakland a couple of weeks ago, I stopped at Detroit. I was traveling in a private car, put at my disposal by a generous Christian manufacturer. While my car was in the yards, I went downtown and addressed a group at a mission. As I finished, an old couple came up, and said, 'Mr. Hadley, won't you go home and take supper with us?'

"I replied, 'You must excuse me; I am not at all well, and it is a great strain for me to go out and visit between meetings. I had better go back to the car and rest.'

"They were so disappointed. The mother faltered. 'Oh, Mr. Hadley, we did want to see you so badly about something.'

"Very well, give me a few moments to lie down and I will go with you."

He then told how they sat together in the old-fashioned parlor, on the horse-hair furniture, and talked. They told him their story: "Mr. Hadley, you know we have a son, Jim. Our son was brought up to go to Sunday school and church, and oh, we had such hopes of him. But he had to work out rather early in life and he got into association with worldly men, and went down and down and down. By and by he came under the power of strong drink. We shall never forget the first time he came home drunk. Sometimes he would never get home at all until the early hours of the morning. Our hearts were breaking over him. One time he did not come all night, but early in the morning, after we had waited through a sleepless night for him, he came in hurriedly, with a pale face, and said, 'Folks, I cannot stay; I must get out. I did something when I was drunk last night, and if it is found out, it will go hard with me. I am not going to stay here and blot your name.' He kissed us both and left, and until recently we have never seen nor heard of him."

"Mr. Hadley, here is a letter that just came from a friend who lives in California, and he tells us, 'I am quite certain that I saw your son, Jim, in San Francisco. I was coming down on a street car, and saw him waiting for a car. I was carried by a block. I hurried back, but he had boarded another car and was gone. I know it was Jim.'

"He is still living, Mr. Hadley, and we are praying that God will save him yet. You are going to California to have meetings out there. Daily we will be kneeling here praying that God will send our boy, Jim, to hear you, and perhaps when he learns how God saved one poor drunkard, he will know there is hope also for him. Will you join us in daily prayer?"

"I said I would, and we prayed together. They made me promise that every day at a given hour, Detroit time, I would lift my heart to God in fellowship with them, knowing that they were kneeling in that room, praying God that He would reach Jim, and give me the opportunity of bringing him to Christ. That was two weeks ago. I have kept my promise every day. My friends, this is my first meeting in California, and here is Jim. Tonight he was drinking in a saloon on Broadway as the great procession passed. He heard the singing, followed us to the theatre, and said, 'I believe I will go in.' He hurried up here, but it was too late. Every place was filled, and the police officer said, 'We cannot allow another person to go inside.' Jim thought, 'This is just my luck. Even if I want to go and hear the gospel, I cannot. I will go

back to the saloon.' He started back; then he returned
determined to see if there was not some way to get in.
He came in the back door, and finally sat in my own
chair. Friends, Jim wants Christ, and I ask you all to
pray for him."

There that night we saw that poor fellow drop on his
knees, and confess his sin and guilt, and accept Christ
as his Saviour. The last sight we had of Jim was when
J. Wilbur Chapman and he were on their way to the
Western Union Telegraph office to send the joyful message: "God heard your prayers. My soul is saved." Oh,
what a God, lover of sinners that He is! How He delights
to reach the lost and needy!

"He Delighteth in Mercy"

This same God was watching over Onesimus. He saw
him when he stole that money, and as he fled from his
master's house. He watched him on his way to Rome,
and in due time brought him face to face with Paul.
Through that same precious gospel that had been blest
to the salvation of Philemon, Onesimus, the thieving
runaway slave, was also saved, and another star was added
to the Redeemer's crown.

Then I can imagine Onesimus coming to Paul, and
saying, "Now, Paul, I want your advice. There is a matter
which is troubling me. You know my master, Philemon.
I must confess that I robbed him and ran away. I feel
now that I must go back, and try to make things right."

One evidence that people are really born of God is
their effort to make restitution for wrong done in the
past. They want a good conscience both before God and
man.

"Paul, ought I to go back in accordance with the
Roman law? I have nothing to pay, and I don't know just

what to do. I do not belong to myself, and it is quite impossible to ever earn anything to make up for the loss. Will you advise me what to do?"

Paul might have said, "I know Philemon well. He has a tender, kind, loving heart and a forgiving spirit. I will write him a note and ask him to forgive you, and that will make everything all right."

But he did not do that. Why? I think that he wanted to give us a wonderful picture of the great gospel of vicarious substitution. One of the primary aspects of the work of the Cross is substitution. The Lord Jesus Christ Himself paid the debt that we owe to the infinite God, in order that when forgiveness came to us it would be on a perfectly righteous basis. Paul, who had himself been justified through the Cross, now says, "I will write a letter to Philemon, and undertake to become your surety. You go back to Philemon, and present my letter. You do not need to plead your own case; just give him my letter."

We see Onesimus with that message from Paul safely hidden in his wallet, hurrying back to Colosse. Imagine Philemon standing on the portico of his beautiful residence, looking down the road, and suddenly exclaiming, "Why, who is that? It certainly looks like that scoundrel, Onesimus! But surely he would not have the face to come back. Still, it looks very much like him. I will just watch and wait."

A little later, he says, "I declare, it *is* Onesimus! He seems to be coming to the house. I suppose he has had a hard time in the world. The stolen money is all gone, and now perhaps he is coming to beg for pardon."

As he comes up the pathway, Onesimus calls, "Master, Master!"

"Well, Onesimus, are you home again?"

"Yes, Master, read this, please."

132 Charge That to My Account

No other word would Onesimus speak for himself; Paul's letter would explain all.

Philemon takes the letter, opens it, and begins to read: *Paul, a prisoner of Jesus Christ.*

"Why Onesimus, where did you meet Paul? Did you see him personally?"

"Yes, Master, in the prison in Rome; he led me to Christ."

Unto Philemon our dearly beloved, and fellow-labourer.

"Little enough I have ever done, but that is just like Paul."

And to our beloved Apphia. (That was Mrs. Philemon.)

"Come here, Apphia. Here is a letter from Paul." When Mrs. Philemon sees Onesimus, she exclaims, "Are you back?"

One can imagine her mingled disgust and indignation as she sees him standing there. But Philemon says: "Yes, my dear, not a word. Here is a letter for us to read—a letter from Paul."

Running on down the letter he comes to this: *Yet for love's sake I rather beseech thee, being such an one as Paul the aged, and now also a prisoner of Jesus Christ. I beseech thee for my son Onesimus.*

"Think of that! He must have been putting it over on Paul in some way or another."

Whom I have begotten in my bonds. "I wonder if he told him anything about the money he stole from us. I suppose he has been playing the religious game with Paul."

Which in time past was to thee unprofitable.

"I should say he was."

But now profitable to thee and to me.

"I am not so sure of that."

Whom I have sent again.

"Paul must have thought a lot of him. If he didn't serve him any better than he did me, he would not get much out of him." He goes on reading through the letter.

"Well, well, that rascally, thieving liar! Maybe Paul believes that he is saved, but I will never believe it unless I find out that he owned up to the wrong he did me."

What is this? *If he hath wronged thee, or oweth thee ought, put that on mine account; I Paul have written it with mine own hand, I will repay it: albeit I do not say to thee how thou owest unto me even thine own self besides.*

Oh, I think in a moment Philemon was conquered. "Why," he says, "it is all out then. He has confessed his sin. He has acknowledged his thieving, owned his guilt, and, just think, Paul, that dear servant of God, suffering in prison for Christ's sake, says: *Put that on my account.* Paul becomes his "surety." It was just as though Paul should write today: "Charge that to my account!"

A Gospel Picture

Is not this a picture of the gospel? A picture of what the Saviour has done for every repentant soul? I think I see Him as he brings the needy, penitent sinner into the presence of God, and says, "My Father, he has wronged Thee, he owes Thee much, but all has been charged to My account. Let him go free." How could the Father turn aside the prayer of His Son after that death of shame and sorrow on Calvary's cross, when He took our blame upon Himself and suffered in our stead?

But now observe it is not only that Paul offered to become Onesimus' surety, it was not merely that he offered to settle everything for Onesimus in regard to the past, but he provided for his future too. He says to Philemon: *"If thou count me therefore a partner, receive him as myself."*

Is not that another aspect of our salvation? We are "accepted in the beloved." The blessed Saviour brings the redeemed one into the presence of the Father, and says, "My Father, if thou countest Me the partner of Thy throne, receive him as Myself." Paul says, *"Not now as a servant, but above a servant, a brother beloved, specially to me, but how much more unto thee, both in the flesh, and in the Lord?"* He is to take the place, not of a bondsman, but of an honored member of the family and a brother in Christ. Think of it—once a poor, thieving, runaway slave, and now a recognized servant of Christ, made welcome for Paul's sake. Thus our Father saves the lawless, guilty sinner, and makes him welcome for Jesus' sake, treating him as He treats His own beloved Son.

> "Jesus paid it all,
>   All to Him I owe;
> Sin had left a crimson stain:
>   He washed it white as snow."

And now every redeemed one is "in Christ before God—yea, made the righteousness of God in him." Oh, wondrous love! Justice is satisfied. What a picture we have here then of substitution and acceptance. The apostle Paul epitomized it all for us: "Who was delivered for our offences, and was raised again for our justification" (Rom. 4:25).

We are accepted in the Beloved. The Lord Jesus became our Surety, settled for all our past, and has provided for all our future. In the Book of Proverbs (11:15), there is a very striking statement, "He that is surety for a stranger shall smart for it; and he that hateth suretyship

is sure." These words were written centuries before the
Cross, to warn men of what is still a very common ground
for failure and ruin in business life. To go surety for a
stranger is a very dangerous thing, as thousands have
learned to their sorrow. It is poor policy to take such a
risk unless you are prepared to lose.

But there was One who knew to the full what all the
consequences of His act would be, and yet, in grace,
deigned to become "surety for a stranger." Meditate upon
these wonderful words: "For ye know the grace of our
Lord Jesus Christ, that, though he was rich, yet for your
sakes he became poor, that ye through his poverty might
be rich" (II Cor. 8:9). He was the stranger's Surety.

A surety is one who stands good for another. Many
a man will do this for a friend, long known and trusted;
but no wise man will so act for a stranger, unless he is
prepared to lose. But it was when we were strangers and
foreigners and enemies, and alienated in our minds by
wicked works, that Jesus in grace became our Surety.
"Christ also hath once suffered for sins, the just for the
unjust, that he might bring us to God."

All we owed was exacted from Him when He suffered
upon the tree for sins not His own. He could then say,
"I restored that which I took not away" (Ps. 69:4). Bishop
Lowth's beautiful rendering of Isaiah 53:7 reads: "It was
exacted and He became answerable." This is the very
essence of the Gospel message. He died in my place; He
paid my debt.

How fully He proved the truth of the words quoted
from Proverbs, when He suffered on that cross of shame!
How He had to "smart for it" when God's awful judgment
against sin fell upon Him. But He wavered not! In love
to God and to the strangers whose Surety He had become, "He endured the cross, despising the shame."

His sorrows are now forever past. He has paid the

debt, met every claim in perfect righteousness. The believing sinner is cleared of every charge, and God is fully glorified.

> "He bore on the tree
>   The sentence for me,
> And now both the Surety
>   And sinner are free."

None other could have met the claims of God's holiness against the sinner and have come out triumphant at last. He alone could atone for sin. Because He has settled every claim, God has raised Him from the dead, and seated Him at His own right hand in highest glory.

Have you trusted "the stranger's surety"? If not, turn to Him now while grace is free.

13

The Way to the City

"The labour of the foolish wearieth
every one of them, because he
knoweth not how to go to the
city" (Eccles. 10:15).

In some respects the Book of Ecclesiastes is the saddest in all the Bible. It gives the search of the natural man for the supreme good under the sun, leading at last only to bitter disappointment and the heart-broken cry: "Vanity of vanities; all is vanity ... all is vanity and vexation of spirit" (1:2, 14).

In this book, Solomon uses a very striking figure. He imagines a countryman on his way to the city, desiring to go perhaps to the great capital of Palestine — Jerusalem, or to some other city upon which his heart is set. But that man starts out trying to find his way with neither guide-post to direct him, nor authoritative information to tell him which route to take. He tries first one road and then another, only to be disappointed every time, until at last, utterly wearied, he throws himself down in despair as the shades of night are falling, and says, "It is no use, I cannot make it; I cannot find my way." "The labour of the foolish wearieth every one of them, because he knoweth not how to go to the city."

If we think of that city as heaven, or as the glorious New Jerusalem, then indeed we may see how aptly Solomon's words apply to myriads of mankind about us. Speak to men about their hope of heaven and they will say uncertainly, "Oh, yes, I trust I shall enter heaven when earth's short day is over; I hope I shall find my way to the city of God; I hope that some day my feet will walk the gold-paved street of the New Jerusalem." If you ask them what assurance they have that they are really on the road that leads to heaven, you will find that they are all in confusion. Many of them will not even thank you for trying to give them authoritative information from the Word of God. Instead of "Thus saith the Lord," you will find them substituting, "I think." What a common thing it is to hear men say, "I think that everything will come out all right in the end; there are many different roads to eternity, many men of many minds, but we are all going to the same place at last; every road will eventually lead to heaven, we hope." But you know that this is not logical, it is not reasonable. It is a principle that does not work in this life, nor in this world, and what reason have we to believe that it will work when we come to another life, and another world?

The Wrong Train

I remember one day leaving Los Angeles by train to go to San Diego. Shortly after we passed Fullerton, my attention was directed to an altercation going on near me. I had observed a little old lady who got on at a station some miles back. My attention was drawn to her because of the great number of bundles she carried. In one hand she had a cage, evidently containing a parrot, some kind of a package held by one finger, a grip, and a bag; but she got in and put them all down about her, and filled the entire space where she sat. She was nicely settled when the conductor came around, and said, "Tickets, please." She handed him her ticket, and he said, "Madam, this is not your train. Your ticket calls for San Bernardino, and you are on the train that goes to San Diego."

"You needn't tell me that," she replied; "I asked a man before I got on, and he told me that this train was going to San Bernardino."

"Well," he said, "I am sorry, but you have been the victim of some wrong information, for this train is going to San Diego."

"I don't believe it," she said; "I bought this ticket in good faith, and have taken the train they told me to take."

"Pardon me," he replied, "but I am the conductor on this train, and it is going to San Diego. If you want to go to San Bernardino, you will have to get off and take a train back."

Finally as the train drew near to the next stop, she gathered up her parrot and her packages and bags, declaring that this was an outrage, and that she would report it to the company and have the conductor discharged for putting her off the train. She left, while the rest of the passengers smiled even though they felt sorry for her.

It is not true that if you take a train going north, you will land somewhere in the south. It is not true that if you are on the road leading to everlasting judgment, you will reach heaven. "The labour of the foolish wearieth every one of them, because he knoweth not how to go to the city."

Well Marked Roads

How grateful are those who have done much motoring for the wonderful way in which the various automobile associations, and also the state and federal governments, have marked the roads all over this great country. We start off in our cars, and every little while we see the signs directing us. When we come to a fork in the road, we are careful to take the right one. But sometimes you get into a region where the roads have not been marked, and how perplexing it often is.

I remember the time we were going from Elizabeth, New Jersey, to California. We were way out in Arizona, and came to a fork in the road. There had been a sign there, but some young vandals had evidently used it as a mark for shooting, and had shot it up so completely that we could not make anything out of it. My secretary, the young man who was driving, said, "I think this is the right road," but I said, "No, I think this is the one." Our thoughts did not amount to anything. We went wrong and got far out of our route, and had to retrace our way many long miles. The labor of the foolish wearied us. Why? Because we did not know the way to the city, we had no authoritative information. How many eternity-bound men and women are content to go on just like that! What egregious folly when God's Word has so plainly marked out the only right way!

Several Wrong Roads

May I indicate some of the roads which men and women take, and which they think will lead them to heaven?

First, there is *Legality Lane*. Do you know that lane? It is a hard, stone road, and many imagine that it will

get them through to heaven. As you pass along you see
the frowning cliffs of Mt. Sinai, you hear the heavy thun-
derings and see the lightning flashing, and you can almost hear the words: "Cursed is every one that continueth
not in all things which are written in the book of the law
to do them."

But you say, "I will do my best; I will try to keep
God's holy commands; I will surely get to heaven at
last." Beware, for *Legality Lane* will bring you eventually to the place of the curse, for God's Word declares
that if a man shall "keep the whole law, and yet offend
in one point, he is guilty of all" (James 2:10). Again we
read, "Cursed is every one that continueth not in all
things which are written in the book of the law to do
them" (Gal. 3:10). No man was ever justified by the works
of the law, and no man ever will be. It is utterly impossible that man should wash out the stains of sin by obedience to that holy law. The law tells you how to behave,
but it does not tell you what to do if you have already
failed and become guilty before God. *Legality Lane* will
never lead you to the New Jerusalem.

Then says some one, "I will try *Reformation Alley*.
It is true I have failed; I have been guilty of many gross
violations of God's law; I have sinned, but I will turn
over a new leaf, begin henceforth to please God, put
away my bad habits, cultivate good ones, and surely all
this will bring me at length to heaven." But my friend,
this road will lead you eventually to eternal disappointment too, for there is a solemn word found in this same
book that reads like this, "God requireth that which is
past" (Eccles. 3:15). Even though you were to reform
today, even though you were to turn over a new leaf and
never have another black mark upon the books, the old
leaves with all their sinful record are still there, and you
will have to face them in the day of judgment, unless

some means shall be found whereby those marks can be blotted out.

"God requireth that which is past." Your grocer does that, you know, and it is perfectly right that he should. You run up a bill for a month or two, and then say, "Dear me, this will never do; this buying on credit is too easy a way to get head over heels in debt. I am going to begin to pay cash for everything I buy." And so you go down to the grocer with your market basket, and say "I am determined to turn over a new leaf."

"In what regard?" the grocer asks.

"I have concluded that this buying on credit is all a mistake, and henceforth I am going to pay cash."

"I am delighted to hear that," he replies, "and when will you be able to settle your old bill?"

"Oh," you say, "you don't understand. I am going to pay cash from now on. Surely you won't hold the old account against me."

"I cannot afford to do business that way," he replies; "you received the groceries from me, and I will expect you to pay for them."

"But if I tell you that I am sorry, and pay you as I buy in the future, surely that ought to satisfy you." But he answers, "I will be delighted to have you as a cash customer, but business makes it necessary that I should require that which is past."

My friend, you may reform, you may turn over a new leaf, but when you get to the end of *Reformation Alley,* you will find that you have landed in a district called Eternal Disappointment, where you hear the sad voice of the Son of God saying: "Depart from me, I never knew you."

There is another highway that runs very close along side this one, it is called *Morality Road.* Many excellent people travel along this way. People whom you would be glad to have in your home, travel this road. You would find pleasure in their society. They are people who eschew all kinds of evil behavior, and pride themselves upon their morals and their ethics. They are what the world calls "good people," but they have no place in their thinking for the Lord Jesus Christ; and yet the Word of God declares: "There is none other name under heaven given among men, whereby we must be saved," but the name of Jesus. My friend, if morals could have saved, if ethics could have fitted you for heaven, Jesus Christ would never have died on Calvary's cross. Down in Gethsemane's garden He cried in the agony of His soul, "O my Father, if it be possible, let this cup pass from me," and if there had been any other way of saving sinners than through His sacrificial death, it would then have been made known.

Right by the side of Morality Road runs *Self-righteousness Boulevard*. It is a magnificent boulevard indeed, and here the scribes and Pharisees and many church dignitaries walk. Listen to one of them crooning his own perfections, as he cries, "I thank God I am not as other men. I am not a drunkard, I am not a blasphemer, I am not an adulterer; I fast twice in the week, I give tithes of all that I possess. Surely if any one gets to heaven I will." But hear the solemn declaration of the Word of God, "All our righteousnesses are as filthy rags." And that expression, *filthy rags,* does not mean shreds of clothing that have been contaminated by the dirt of the streets, but it refers to robes tainted and made unclean through the inward corruption that has exuded from the sores of lepers. Naaman, the leper, wearing his magnificent robes might throw off one of these garments, and say, "Look, I want to make you a gift, take this." Would you thank him for the gift? No, you would say, "Keep it away from me, it is contaminated by the leprosy from within." That is what our own righteousnesses are like. They all come from a corrupt, evil heart, and therefore, they can never justify a guilty sinner before God. The end of *Self-righteousness Boulevard* is the lake of fire.

And then akin to this is another road that we will call *Ritualistic Avenue.* Did you ever meet any one on that road? I said to a young lady one day, "I am glad to see you in the meeting; are you a Christian?"

"Yes," she said, "I have been a member of such and such a church ever since I was a child."

"Pardon me," I said, "but you did not understand my question. Have you ever been born again?"

"I was baptized when I was only eight days old," she replied.

"You don't understand me yet," I said, "were you ever converted?"

"Oh, yes," she said, "I was confirmed when I was twelve years of age, and took the sacrament for the first time, and I have been very careful to attend services and take the sacrament ever since. You can be sure I am all right."

She was flitting down *Ritualistic Avenue* imagining it was the road to heaven when it was really leading her as fast as time could carry her to the pit of the abyss, and if not saved, she would plunge over the cliff of time into the darkness of eternity only to find out that baptism cannot save, sacraments cannot save, church-joining cannot save. It is Jesus only that washes away sin and fits us for glory.

Then there is another popular road that many take today. It is called *Delusion Road.* The people on this road are those who will not have the simple gospel of this Book, they will not take the plain statements of the Bible as to the deity of our Lord Jesus Christ, as to His sacrificial atoning death on the cross, but are ready to listen to every kind of folly. As they go down that road you hear them muttering to themselves, "God is all and all is God." "God is good and good is God." "There is no such thing as evil and sin and death." "Every day, in every way, I am growing better and better."

Men are deluding themselves, shutting their eyes to the realities of life. Aristotle, the great Greek philosopher, was wiser than they, for he said, "If any man rejects the testimony of the five senses, there is nothing else on which to build." What can you do for a man who is suffering from the twinges of rheumatism, but who looks at you, and says, "There is no such thing as pain, no such thing as suffering." Or, a man who can be a victim of all kinds of sinful habits, and yet looks you in the eye, and says, "There is no such thing as sin." Or, a man who can stand by the body of a dead loved one, and say, "There is no such thing as death"?

Scripture affirms, "Woe unto them that call evil good, and good evil; that put darkness for light, and light for darkness; that put bitter for sweet, and sweet for bitter!" (Isa. 5:20). *Delusion Road* will end at last in an eternal hell, and men will wake up too late to find out that sin is a reality, that death is a reality, that heaven is a reality and they have missed it, that hell is a reality and it is to be their place of abode forever. What a fearful thing it is to turn from God and trust in fables, to turn away from the sign-post that God has given to point the way to the city of God and take the opposite direction, hoping to reach heaven at last. "If therefore the light that is in thee be darkness, how great is that darkness!" (Matt. 6:23).

The Modernism Way

Another road is called *Modern Thought Highway*. Many of the intelligensia tread that path. It is dotted with universities and schools of higher education, and we find people peddling books up and down this highway, for the folk on this road are the learned of this world. They are too proud to accept, "Thus saith the Lord," but bow down before science, before modern thought, before philosophy, and all the different delusions that are turning men away from God. Let me read you the testimony of a man who admits that he is treading this road. It is written by Professor Melinowski:

> "Personally, I am an agnostic. That is, I am not able to deny the existence of God: nor would I be inclined to do so, still less to maintain that such a belief is not necessary. I also fervently hope that there is a survival after death, and I deeply desire to obtain some certainty on this matter. But with all that, I am unable to accept any positive religion—Christian or otherwise. I cannot positively believe in Providence in any sense of the word, and I have no conviction of personal immortality."

In other words, this man says, "I should like to go to the city of God, if there be such a city. I should like to spend my eternity there. But I cannot trust the Guide Book, I cannot believe the sign-post, I cannot put my confidence in One who says He came from there and went back, and is Himself the Way there." Yet this man is a great deal more modest than many who tread this road. He goes on to say:

> "Thus, as you see, I profoundly differ from the confident rationalist or disbeliever of the past generation or two. We all know the story of La Place and the discussion which he had with Napoleon the First about his system of Celestial Mechanics. The Emperor asked him: 'What place have you given to God in your system?' 'Sire,' was the answer, 'this is an hypothesis of which I have never felt the need.' It is the proud answer of a confident atheist, but it does not ring true to the humble agnostic."

Men today will tell you frankly, "I never felt the need of God; I do not need Him now, and I do not feel there will be need for Him in eternity." But Melinowski continues:

"On the contrary, I should say that God is a reality and not a hypothesis, and a reality of which I am in the greatest need, though this need I cannot satisfy or fulfill. The typical rationalist says: 'I don't know, and I don't care.' The tragic agnostic would rejoin: 'I cannot know, but I feel a deep and passionate need of faith, of evidence, and of revelation.' Personally, to me, and to those many who are like me, nothing really matters except the answer to the burning questions: 'Am I going to live, or shall I vanish like a bubble? What is the aim, and the sense, and the issue of all this strife and suffering?' The doubt of these two questions lives in us, and affect all our thoughts and feelings. Modern agnosticism is a tragic and shattering frame of mind. To dismiss agnosticism as an easy and shallow escape from the moral obligations and discipline of religion—this is an unworthy and superficial way of dealing with it. Is science responsible for my agnosticism and for that of others who think like me? I believe it is, and therefore I do not love science, though I have to remain its loyal servant. Is there any hope of bridging this deepest gulf between tragic agnosticism and belief? I do not know. Is there any remedy? I cannot answer this either."

The blessed, holy Word of God answers every one of these questions, but the modern mind turns away from it all, and says, "No, I would rather go on questioning, go on in uncertainty, than to face the problem of Jesus Christ."

But Jesus Christ is not a problem, He is the *solution* to every problem for life, for death, and for eternity. Listen to the poor woman at the well. Wonderingly she gazes at the Jewish stranger who seems so ready to deal graciously with the Samaritan, and she says, "I know that Messias cometh, which is called Christ: when he is come, he will tell us all things." Oh, the questions that were welling up in that woman's heart — "If I could only see Him maybe He would answer all my questions, maybe He would solve all my problems," and quietly, earnestly, kindly, Jesus looks upon her, and says, "I that speak unto thee am he." She took one long look into those fathomless eyes of His, and in a moment every question was answered, and back to the city she ran, and said to the men, "Come, see a man, which told me all things that ever I did: is not this the Christ?" Yes, He is the answer to every problem.

You remember it is written in Proverbs 14:12, "There is a way which seemeth right unto a man, but the end thereof are the ways of death." All these different pathways which have been indicated are the ways that seem right to man, but end in outer darkness. When Thomas asked the question, "Lord, how can we know the way?" Jesus answered, "I am the way, the truth, and the life: no man cometh unto the Father, but by me" (John 14:6).

Do you want to know the way to the city? Jesus is the Way. Do you want to know the truth in regard to the great problems of time and eternity? Jesus is the Truth. Do you want to know where life is found, so that you may be a new creature? Jesus is the Life. And, "He that believeth on the Son hath everlasting life: and he that believeth not the Son shall not see life; but the wrath of God abideth on him" (John 3:36). My friend, surely you want to find the way to the City. When at last you lie down and say good-by to your friends and loved ones, surely you want to be able to say, as one dear saint of God did, "Earth is receding and heaven is opening." If you do, you need Christ, for He alone is the Way to the city of God, and He says, "him that cometh to me

I will in no wise cast out" (John 6:37). Are you saying, "I should like to find the way, I should like to know Christ, but how may I make His acquaintance?"

> "If I ask Him to receive me,
>   Will He say me nay?
> Not 'till earth and not 'till heaven,
>   Pass away."

If you will come as a sinner, confessing your guilt, forsaking every other refuge, and put your trust in Him alone, He will save you according to His Word, and you shall know Him as the only Way that leads to

> "Jerusalem, the golden,
> With milk and honey blest."

14
The Chains of Sin

"And he smote Peter on the side, and raised him up, saying, Arise up quickly. And his chains fell off from his hands" (Acts 12:7).

Let me draw your attention to a most interesting incident, recorded in Acts 12:1-19. However, I do not intend to consider it from a merely historical standpoint, but as a remarkable illustration of man's lost condition, and God's marvelous salvation. I want you to think of Peter, not as an apostle, nor as an eminent servant of Christ, but as a picture of any poor lost sinner. We notice six things predicated of Peter which are true of every unconverted man.

First, we see him in *bondage*. He is captive to a tyrant, determined upon his destruction. Are you out of Christ, and do you think that you are free, and sometimes look with pity upon Christians because you imagine they are in bondage to certain ancient ideas which keep them from enjoying themselves in the world, the way you fancy you are enjoying yourself? The Jews of Christ's day boldly declared that they were never in bondage to any man, but Jesus said, "The servant of sin is the slave of sin." They were in bondage to sin and Satan, and that is true of every unconverted person. The unbeliever is deceived by the devil; he is captive to his will. You may say, "I am not going to give up my will to some one else," but you have already done that very thing. If you are unsaved, you are a captive to the god and prince of this world, and what is more you cannot deliver yourself, you cannot set yourself free.

In the second place, Peter was *guarded*. Herod had guards stationed to watch and see that he did not get away. He was delivered to four quaternions of soldiers. I do not know the actual names of those soldiers, but I have an idea of what they suggest. One of them might suggest *pride,* another *procrastination,* a third, *sinful pleasure,* and the last, *the love of the world;* for I know that these are the means that Satan uses to guard men, and keep them in their sins, and hinder them from getting deliverance. How many there are who would have come to Christ years ago but for the pride of the human heart — too proud to acknowledge their lost condition, to confess their sins, to admit their wrong. "Pride goeth before destruction, and a haughty spirit before a fall."

The Indian Prince

I heard a story years ago which illustrates the folly of pride.

There were two Hindu princes in conflict one with another. One had been defeated, and his son taken captive. The victorious Rajah was going to march into the city in triumph, with a great string of captives walking barefoot before the great elephant upon which he was mounted. This young prince was brought before him, and told that he was to strip off his royal garments and walk barefoot with the other captives. He was very indignant, and exclaimed, "What kind of faces will the people make when they see me, a prince, walking like that?"

"You have not yet heard it all," said the Rajah, "you shall not only walk barefoot in this procession, but you will carry a bowl of milk that will be filled almost to the brim, and if you spill one drop of it, off comes your head. I shall have guards to see whether you spill any or not."

The prince turned deadly pale as he heard that. As the procession was arranged, they handed him the bowl of milk. You can imagine his predicament. The procession started. How carefully this young prince walked! But in some way or another he managed to get through without spilling a drop. When he was brought before the Rajah, he was sternly asked: "Well, what kind of faces did the people make?"

"O sire," said the poor prince, "I saw no one's face; I saw only my life that I held in my hands, and I knew that if I dared to look to the right or to the left, it would be forfeited."

O friend, you are a poor sinner exposed to the judgment of God, but now offered a free and full salvation through infinite grace. Are you too proud to be saved on God's terms, too proud to humble yourself and admit your lost condition? Are you more concerned about what men think than what God thinks? How well the devil knows how to guard his subjects!

Other Prison Guards

Then there is that other guard, *procrastination.* "The road of By-and-By leads to the town of Never." A great many people are not saved, because they are always saying, "There is plenty of time," and the devil puts old Captain Procrastination on duty to guard them, and if they get exercised, he says to the young, "There is plenty of time; you are young yet." To those in middle life, he says, "Go on and make your fortune, then you can think about your soul." But old age comes and they are still in their sins. The time for them is gone, and they pass into eternity—lost. "The harvest is past, the summer is ended, and we are not saved" (Jer. 8:20).

How well Satan knows how to use the third and fourth guards—*the pleasures of sin* and *the love of the world*—to keep people from coming to Christ. If they bestir themselves and are anxious to be saved, these guards are there to say, "You will lose all your good times, if you become a Christian; you will have to be long-faced and you will be miserable and wretched. You won't be able to go to this, or to that; you won't be able to enjoy this or that; put it off; wait until the world has lost its charm." And so, because men love the world and think more of the pleasures of sin than they do of their eternal salvation, they remain in bondage—some of them until it is too late to be saved.

Peter's Dire Condition

Then notice the third thing: Peter was in *darkness.* That is the condition of every one by nature: "Having the understanding darkened, being alienated from the life of God through the ignorance that is in them, because of the blindness of their heart" (Eph. 4:18). You cannot see in the dark. How often you will hear this said, "I have heard of this salvation for years, but I cannot see how God can save a sinner through the death of His Son; I cannot see how the blood of Christ can wash away my guilt; I cannot understand how I can be sure that the

Bible is the Word of God." Of course you cannot! You are in darkness, and what you need is light. The great apostle to the Gentiles declares, "But if our gospel be hid, it is hid to them that are lost: In whom the god of this world hath blinded the minds of them which believe not, lest the light of the glorious gospel of Christ, who is the image of God, should shine unto them" (II Cor. 4:3, 4). If you make the confession, "I cannot see; I cannot understand how the blood of Jesus can wash away my sin," that is all that is needed to tell the true condition of your soul. You are in the dark, away from God, and in dire need of a Saviour.

Then notice something else: Peter was not only in bondage, guarded, and in darkness, but he was *sound asleep.* That is the condition of men in their sins today. But the voice of God sounds forth: "Awake thou that sleepest, and arise from the dead, and Christ shall give thee light" (Eph. 5:14). The business of the evangelist is to go to men, asleep in their sins, and awaken them. Real hard sleepers do not like to be awakened. I have two boys, and both of them, when they were at a certain growing age, did like to stay up late at night; but oh, how hard it was to get them up in the morning! What a job it was to awaken them. Listen to the sleeper in Proverbs, "Yet a little sleep, a little slumber, a little folding of the hands to sleep" (Prov. 6:10). My friend, a little more sleep and you will awaken in hell to sleep no more for all eternity! It is only the omnipotent power of God that can awaken poor sleeping sinners.

Then there is something else: Peter was *bound* with two chains. Are you bound with the chains of your sin? You may remember the story of the Grecian tyrant, who looked with suspicion upon a certain metal worker, who was able to make the finest chains of any man in his dominions. This tyrant had an idea that the man was a traitor against his government. One day he sent for him, and after flattering him, said, "I understand there is no one in my kingdom that can make as fine or as strong a chain as you can. Let me see you make one." With the tyrant looking on, the smith made a magnificent chain. He finished it, and as he handed it over to the tyrant, he said, "If you were to take two elephants, and fasten one to each end of this chain, they could not tear it apart."

The tyrant said, "Are you certain of that?"

"Absolutely," the man replied.

Then, turning to two of his officers, the tyrant said, "Take him and bind him with it, and cast him into prison." He was bound with the very chain he had made.

Sinner, you have been forging a chain, the chain of your sins, link by link throughout the years, and if you are not saved soon, you are going to be bound with that chain, and be cast into that awful place "prepared for the devil and his angels." You will have no one to blame but yourself. You will remember how you forged that chain, link by link; how you fell into this or that particular sin, and then said to yourself, "Oh, well, I will not repeat it; I will do it just once." Then in some way there was an unaccountable urge to commit the same sin again and again and again, and you found out at last that you were forging the links in the chain that has bound your soul. You have tried and tried to break it, but you are not able to do it.

Chains that Bind

You know what chains are binding *your* soul today. The awful chains of lust, untruthfulness, pride, infidelity, dishonesty, greed, and unbelief. These are the things that are going to bind men's souls for eternity, and sink them down into outer darkness. It is said of the fallen angels that they are bound in everlasting chains under darkness; and that will be true also of men and women who reject Christ.

The chains of sin! You remember how you tried to break them! On New Year's Day, you said, "Now I am going to swear off; I am not going to commit this sin or that sin any more. I am losing my will-power; these things have robbed me of my self respect; I am ashamed to think of the habits of which no one knows, but myself and God; I will surely break loose." And you tried and tried, and then fell back into the same old ways.

Or, you may have said, "It is of no use to try; I cannot free myself; I am bound with chains that I cannot break." And so far as your own strength is concerned, that is perfectly true. But that is not the whole story. What have we seen of Peter? We have seen that he was a captive; he was guarded by Satan's soldiers; he was wrapped in darkness; he was sound asleep; he was bound with chains; and there is one other word to complete the vivid description, he was under sentence of *death,* condemned already. There he lies in that prison, a picture of any poor sinner.

Why was the sentence against Peter not carried out? Herod was waiting until a more propitious time, when he was going to bring him before the people and put him to death. That suggests what God says about you, if you are still rejecting the Lord Jesus Christ. "He that believeth on him is not condemned: but he that believeth not is condemned already, because he hath not believed in the name of the only begotten Son of God" (John 3:18). Notice, that you are not merely in danger of being condemned in the day of judgment; not only in danger of condemnation, if you die rejecting Christ; but you are *condemned already.* And why? Because you are even now a Christ-rejector. "He that believeth not is condemned already." Again in John 3:36, we read, "He that believeth not on the Son shall not see life; but the wrath of God abideth on him." Just as the wrath of Herod was abiding on Peter, and he was waiting the time for the sentence to be carried out, so the wrath of a righteous God abides upon the Christ-rejector, and soon the sentence will be carried out.

Deliverance Through Prayer

But now a word to Christians: You are interested in sinners, you know they are in the darkness, you understand that they are captives of Satan, bound by the chains of their sins, guarded, and under condemnation, and yet you have a resource, have you not? The people of God offered prayer to God continually for Peter's deliverance. O Christian, be encouraged when you pray for those in bondage. The ear of God is open to your cry. There are dear boys and girls who are still unsaved, and you realize they are in the dark; you long that they should be brought to the light. Keep on praying for them! As the saints prayed for Peter, God wrought; as we pray for sinners, God saves today!

What happened as they prayed for Peter? Seven things took place.

First, as they were praying, a messenger from God came to Peter. You know how often God does just that very thing. Sometimes he sends a human messenger, sometimes a word from the Book, sometimes conviction by the Holy Spirit. Peter was sound asleep, and suddenly there appeared a messenger. The angel of the Lord is able to awaken, to arouse, to give deliverance to those who desire to be delivered.

Second, a light shone in the prison. It is the truth of God that dispels the darkness. "The entrance of thy words giveth light; it giveth understanding unto the simple" (Ps. 119:130). The messenger came, and the light shone! O unsaved sinner, have you heard the gospel message, the message of light? You say in your darkness, "I cannot see; I cannot understand." Listen! "This is a faithful saying, and worthy of all acceptation, that Christ Jesus came into the world to save sinners; of whom I am chief" (I Tim. 1:15). Does that not give you a little light? "Verily, verily, I say unto you, He that heareth my word, and believeth on him that sent me, hath everlasting life, and shall not come into condemnation; but is passed from death unto life" (John 5:24). This is God's own Word. May it bring light to your darkened mind.

Third, the angel smote Peter on the side. He was a real "Billy" Sunday. Some folk do not like "Billy's" abrupt way, but in this case the situation was desperate, and the angel said, "Wake up," as he smote him, and Peter wakened to find the angel pounding him. Some of us remember how the Spirit laid hold on us, and aroused us from our death-like sleep. The Word came home with convicting power, and we were saved. I would to God that you, unsaved one, might be smitten by the convicting power of the Spirit of God, that you might realize your lost condition, and your need of a Saviour; and that you would turn to Him who awakens, and be delivered.

Fourth, there was no resistance on Peter's part. The message came, "Get up!" and Peter obeyed immediately. Why, you know, a little while before, that word would have meant nothing to him; but now he is awake. When men and women are awakened, the message comes: "Believe the Word; arise, He calleth thee."

Fifth, then his chains fell off. Do you want to be delivered from your chains? Believe the Word! I have a friend who years ago was a victim of that dreadful habit of smoking and eating opium. He had fallen into that vice when very young, and the thing had gotten such a grip on him that he could not break it. At last, at twenty-two years of age, he was such a wreck that he had made up his mind that he might as well end it all by suicide, for there was no hope for him. But one night in Fresno, California, he was going down the street, crying out, "What a fool I have been to form a habit like this that I cannot free myself from," when he heard a little group of Salvation Army folk singing,

> "He breaks the power of canceled sin,
>   He sets the prisoner free;
> His blood can make the vilest clean,
>   His blood avails for me."

He said, "What's that?" They sang it again, That poor young fellow stood there trembling, for he had hardly strength enough to stand erect. "I wonder if it is true — 'the vilest' — that's me!" and he followed them into their hall. When they invited sinners to come to Christ, he went forward and knelt at the penitent bench, but he was so loathsome that they said, "Oh, he is too far gone." However, they were faithful, and knelt with him and pointed him to Christ. By and by, as he arose, he said, "I will trust Him," and went away. One of them said to another, "You better go and see if he has any lodging tonight; he has no will power, there is no hope for him, if he gets away." Somebody did take an interest in him; he got him a lodging, and helped him in other ways. When he put his trust in Christ, he was delivered, and he has often testified since, "I am free; Christ has delivered me; I never even had a struggle to get rid of that habit." In two weeks you would not have known him. He was a new creature, physically, mentally, and every way. Whatever your sins are, come to Christ, trust in Him, and find deliverance. Peter's bonds fell off; he was freed from his chains — you too may be free.

Sixth, "Get your things on," the angel said, and he dressed him up. That is what the Lord does. Off with the prison garments, on with the new garments. Then they went through one door and another, and finally through the great iron door. If Peter had gone through that great iron door in his chains, he would have gone through to die. If he were taken through in his fetters, he would go out to be executed. And if you go through the door of death in your sins, you go through to your doom. Peter might well have trembled as he passed through that door, if he still had his chains on; but as he drew near, the door opened of its own accord, and he went through as a free man. A believer in the Lord Jesus can say, "I have died already; I am free!" You may ask, "How can you say that?" "Well, we have been crucified with Christ; we went through death with Him!"

Seventh, then Peter said, "I must hunt up some place where I can find some Christians who are interested in me." They were all having a prayer meeting in Mary's house, praying for Peter's deliverance. The Lord had answered and he was delivered, but they were still praying. A little girl came out in response to Peter's knock, and she got so excited when she heard his voice, that she forgot to open the door. She rushed back, and said, "You don't need to pray any more; Peter is outside, he is at the door!"

"Nonsense," they practically said, "God doesn't do anything as quickly as that."

Is that not just like us? Sometimes we pray and pray, and when God answers, we can hardly believe it. But she insisted, "I *know* he is there."

"It is his ghost," they said, "he has gone through in his chains, and that is his ghost."

"Well," she replied, "there is no use arguing; come and see!" And to the door they went where Peter continued knocking!

What an illustration this is, dear unsaved one, of God's salvation. Have you seen your own picture? Have you been asleep in your sins? Are you in darkness and guarded by Satan? Do you want to be delivered? Listen to the Word of God, and do not be angry if the Spirit of God has to smite you. Believe the Word, act upon it, and you will enter into the fullness of blessing. You will be delivered from the chains of your sins.

The Unchanging Christ

Consistent Christian Behavior

15

Consistent Christian Behavior

"When thou buildest a new house, then thou shalt make a battlement for thy roof, that thou bring not blood upon thine house, if any man fall from thence. Thou shalt not sow thy vineyard with divers seeds; lest the fruit of thy seed which thou hast sown, and the fruit of thy vineyard, be defiled. Thou shalt not plow with an ox and an ass together. Thou shalt not wear a garment of divers sorts, as of woollen and linen together. Thou shalt make thee fringes upon the four quarters of thy vesture, wherewith thou coverest thyself" (Deut. 22:8-12).

As an amplification of the last verse in the above passage, let us turn to Numbers 15:37, 38, where we read: "And the LORD spake unto Moses, saying, Speak unto the children of Israel, and bid them that they make them fringes in the borders of their garments throughout their generations, and that they put upon the fringe of the borders a ribband of blue." The Apostle Paul has set us the example of drawing spiritual lessons from some of these Old Testament regulations for which, otherwise, we might not see the need in our day. When he treats of the support of Christian ministers, he goes back to Deuteronomy to find a text. He selects one that we might think had no real application to the subject in hand—a very peculiar text indeed, "Thou shalt not muzzle the ox that treadeth out the corn." We might naturally ask, What has that to do with the question of the support of a minister of the gospel? But Paul uses it, not to teach consideration for the toiling creatures who so patiently serve man, though this is clearly emphasized in Scripture, but rather to show us our responsibility to care for the temporal needs of spiritual laborers, in order that they may be free to carry on their work without anxiety as to earthly things.

We read in the Book of Proverbs: "A righteous man regardeth the life of his beast; but the tender mercies of the wicked are cruel." A man who had been converted gave his testimony to that fact at a public meeting. When he got through, his wife stepped up, and said, "My friends, if any one here questions my husband's testimony, you should come out to our farm. Before he was converted, every cow, every horse, and every dog on the place would run away from him because he was so vicious and would beat them so cruelly; now, all the animals run to him." The man's whole attitude toward the creatures of the farm was changed. But the Apostle Paul says that this was not written just for the oxen, but for our benefit. The oxen treading out the corn is a beautiful picture of the servant of Christ—beating out the soul-nourishing truth of the Word of God in order that he may pass it on to us. Now think of the ox treading out the corn, and reaching down every now and then to pick up a bite for himself. God says, that they who preach the gospel should live of the gospel. Too many churches forget that. They are quite content to have the servants of Christ minister the Word year in and year out, and are not concerned in the least as to how they are cared for. They are like the deacon who prayed, "Lord, bless our minister; keep him humble, and we will keep him poor." The apostle's use of that text suggests many texts applying to by-gone conditions, which, after all, have a hidden suggestion for us.

These five verses in Deuteronomy prove this in a remarkable way. "When thou buildest a new house, then thou shalt make a battlement for thy roof, that thou bring not blood upon thine house, if any man fall from thence." The roofs of the Hebrews' houses, as the roofs of many Oriental houses today, or the roofs of the Pueblo Indians and the Mexicans of our own country, served as places of social intercourse, where the families gathered to visit. The roof answered the same purpose that our living-room does; in fact, the Hebrew could have well called the roof his parlor, a place of communion and fellowship. Samuel took Saul up on the roof and talked to him; he put food before him and bade him eat. The roof also was a place of prayer, for we read that the Apostle Peter was praying on the roof of the house when he received the vision of the sheet which was suspended from heaven—a picture of the mystery of the Church. Sometimes we go too far in saying that the mystery of the Church was revealed only to the Apostle Paul. The "all manner of beasts" represented the Gentiles' right to the gospel, afterward made expressly clear to Paul. God said, "When you build a new house you are to put a battlement around your roof." What for? Lest anybody should fall from thence. But here is a Hebrew who says,

"I don't think a battlement will fit in with my plan of architecture. Besides, my wife and I are both elderly people. There is no danger for either of us. I will make a roof with a straight edge without any battlement." Before long some neighbor comes to visit them. They have a child of tender years, who, in running and playing about on the roof, comes too near the edge and goes over. Why did God order a battlement about the roof? Simply for this reason: the battlement afforded protection for all. This man is held responsible for the death of the child. The battlement may not always be for your own sake, but for the sake of other people. Does it not emphasize the New Testament words, "For none of us liveth to himself, and no man dieth to himself"? A great many things that we, as individuals, think we could do with impunity would wreck the Christian life of somebody weaker in faith. The fact that he sees us do something which he fears is not right or consistent with a Christian profession may lead him to do the same thing, but his consecration does not stand the strain — worldly things soon overcome him and his testimony as a Christian is lost. You can see, therefore, that your example was not right. An evil example has doubtless been the cause of much backsliding. In the eighth chapter of First Corinthians we read of meat being offered to idols. Paul says that the Christian should not eat such meat if it would offend a weak one; we should do nothing to offend one of these. But, you say, "I can take that nice, tender steak. I can eat it and enjoy it even though it has been dedicated to the idol, for I know an idol is nothing but a mere lifeless image." "Yes, I know," says Paul, "but somebody else might drift away from Christianity if he saw you do it. Ruin not him for whom Christ died." We should live for others; we should be willing to sacrifice much in order to help others, and not mislead them.

"Thou shalt not sow thy vineyard with divers seeds: lest the fruit of thy seed which thou hast sown, and the fruit of thy vineyard, be defiled." Seed? For us, that means the Word of God. We have been entrusted with the Word of God, holy and free from error. Thou shalt not use divers seeds. I want to warn you against dabbling with false cults. Some think they must be up-to-date, so they read everything and study everything that they can get their hands on in order that they may be well read. Often doubts are instilled in the mind in regard to great truths of God's Word, all because the vineyard has been sown with mingled seed. Here was Elisha preparing a meal for the sons of the prophets. Finances were not too abundant, so he sent them out into the field to gather some greens for dinner; by mistake, they gathered some that were poisonous. One of the students was a good taster, and it happened that, before they ate, he reached down and tasted *death* in the pot. Elisha was informed of the fact, and the greens were omitted from the menu. One spoonful proved that death was there. Some people think you have to go to the bottom of the pot in order to really test out what is in it. Someone says, "I believe in investigating; I can get a little good out of everything. I look into all religions and I find a little good in all of them. I listen to this one and that one and I can get a little good from all." Suppose we admit that. Our digestive organs might be able to assimilate stewed or boiled sawdust and possibly get a little nourishment from it, if there is any. But what a fool I would be to eat sawdust, when I could get good oatmeal porridge! Why not give yourself that which you know is nourishing? Thou shalt not sow thy vineyard with mingled seed lest it be defiled. That is why the apostle wrote: "Study to shew thyself approved unto God, a workman that needeth not to be ashamed, rightly dividing the word of truth" (II Tim. 2:15).

Have you ever noticed in some preaching an absolute lack of definiteness? I was in a school recently where a man talked very indefinitely. At the close of his message, a youth asked me this question, "Is he a modernist or a fundamentalist?" I had to answer, "I do not know." There was nothing absolutely wrong, yet he did not say anything that any modernist could not have approved; it would not have killed a fly; it didn't amount to anything. Preach the truth in its simplicity. Don't get off on other lines.

The next verse is a warning against the unequal yoke. "Thou shalt not plow with an ox and an ass together." When the apostle wrote, in II Corinthians, "Be ye not unequally yoked together with unbelievers" (6:14), he must have had this passage in mind. An ox and a donkey, unsuited to each other, together—a stalwart old ox and a donkey, an unequal arrangement. Why? The ox is a clean beast, used for sacrifice, and the ass is an unclean beast, a type of the natural man. That is the trouble with all of us; by nature, we are just stubborn donkeys. The donkey nature will come out in us sometimes, even after conversion. We may say that the ass is a type of the sinner, the man in his natural condition; the ox is a picture of the servant of God. "Thou shalt not plow with an ox and an ass together." How far does this go? It touches every relationship in life. A Christian man has an opportunity to buy his way into a well-paying business. It means partnership with an ungodly man. How long does he do business without feeling the yoke galling him? They are not fitted to work together. Such an arrangement generally culminates in the backsliding of the Christian—unless he breaks away. Some think that this does not apply to fraternal relationships. Often when I finish preaching, men will come to me and shake my hand in all kinds of strange ways. Belong to a fraternal organization? I belong to the greatest one on earth! The Church of the living God is a wonderful society—a secret society of the mysteries that the world knows nothing about. Why have I not joined human fraternal organizations? Several scriptures have kept me out. I am to take the Lord Jesus as my example. He said, "In secret I have said nothing." I have to follow Him. Then there is this question of the unequal yoke. And God has said, "Have no fellowship with the unfruitful works of darkness." We belong to the light. What place have we in the secret lodge room?

Then there is the question of Church fellowship. The bane of the professing church is its effort to get numbers. Get the people into the church and afterwards get them converted—build up a church-membership. Where, in God's Word, do you read of the apostles of our Lord trying to get the unsaved into church-fellowship? Where in the Word do you read that you must get the unregenerate in the church first, and then do them good afterwards? Ordinarily it works out as in the case of the boys who caught young linnets and placed one on one side and one on the other side of the canary. They told their mother that they had caught them young and placed them there by the canary so that they would learn to sing as did the canary. The mother was rather dubious, but she did not say anything. A few days later the boys rushed to their mother and cried, "Mother, our canary is chirping like a linnet." The linnets never learned to sing as the canary, but the canary lost its song. Christians become exceedingly worldly by association in church-fellowship with the worldly. Be sure people are saved, and then lead them on into Christian fellowship.

This applies also to the marriage relationship. I never

can understand how a real Christian can contemplate entering into the most sacred of all relationships with an unsaved person. Some seem to imagine that once married, they will be able to lead their partners to Christ. It generally goes the other way. After the honeymoon the unsaved one says, "I am not going to church any more, or have any more of that religious cant in my home." The unsaved one is usually the stronger. The other one has already disobeyed Christ, so he has not much spiritual strength by which to stand. An old Puritan divine once said, "If you marry a child of the devil, you can expect to have trouble with your father-in-law." "Thou shalt not plow with an ox and an ass together."

Here is one that will come home to us, for it is about clothes. "Thou shalt not wear a garment of divers sort, as of woollen and linen together." Isn't it strange that God would not allow His people to wear mixed clothes? It was all right to wear linen and woolen if they were different garments, but not one in which the two were mixed. I want to call your attention to the word "garment" in this verse. In the Bible the word is used in two ways, meaning both clothing and behavior. Also in our English language, as well as in the Bible, garment and behavior are the same word; we have "habit" in clothing and "habit" in behavior. There are walking habits, riding habits, and bathing habits. We say, "That young man has a very evil habit," or "a good habit," meaning, of course, good behavior. Clothing then represents behavior. We speak of someone's garments always being white. What is that? Behavior. "Fine linen" is the righteousnesses of the saints. The Bride has made herself ready by righteous behavior. The sinner's righteousnesses are as filthy rags, just like old, defiled garments. Now God says to you and to me: "You are not to be people of mixed behavior, very pious and godly in the classroom and thoroughly worldly and carnal outside; religious in church and very frivolous and foolish in the world — not to have one behavior in one company and another in another company." Remember, wherever you find yourself, that you are there to represent the Lord Jesus Christ. Take Lot for an example. Lot wore garments of linen and woolen. When with Abraham, he was very saintly, but in Sodom there was not much difference between him and the crowd. He was thought so well of, in fact, that they elected him a judge. They never would have made Abraham a judge.

Let us think for a moment, on worldly pleasures. No Christian who is walking with God is troubled much concerning them. In the first place, the world doesn't want them around. Gypsy Smith, the great evangelist, in a sermon one night, danced across the stage, and then said, "My friends, I can dance as well as any of you, but since the day I was converted, nobody has invited me to a dance or to the theatre." Why hadn't they? Because they knew from the day of his conversion that he was out and out for God! Your conversion has killed your chances with the world. Can't you hear some worldly friend saying, "There isn't any use asking her. She will throw gloom all over the party, talking about our souls. Imagine her getting you into some corner and saying, 'Is your soul saved?' " If you wear the right kind of garments, you will never be in style with the world.

Now we will look at the positive side of this question. "Thou shalt make thee fringes upon the four quarters of thy vesture, wherewith thou coverest thyself." "And the LORD spake unto Moses, saying, Speak unto the children of Israel, and bid them that they make them fringes in the borders of their garments throughout their generations, and that they put upon the fringes of the borders a ribband of blue" (Num. 15:37, 38). The Lord Jesus undoubtedly dressed that way. But why the ribbon of blue? In order "That ye may remember, and do all my commandments, and be holy unto your God" (v. 40). God says to His people, "You are to be characterized by heavenly-mindedness in all your ways." Are you always careful to have the ribbon of blue? Do people realize that you belong to heaven? Our citizenship, you know, is in heaven. "If ye then be risen with Christ, seek those things which are above, where Christ sitteth on the right hand of God. Set your affections on things above, not on things on the earth." The Israelite had this band of blue around the lower edge of his garment (he always wore long flowing garments), so that right down to the very lowest place where the garment nearly touched the earth he wore that which showed he belonged to the God of heaven. Where you and I come closest to the world, we are to manifest the heavenly character. Can you say, "For me to live is Christ"? Who lives Christ? One who wears a ribbon of blue!

It has been told how, years ago, the Crown Prince of France was put under the care of an English tutor. The Dauphin was of royal blood and his tutor was of ordinary strain. It was unthinkable that a commoner should attempt to punish one of royal blood, and yet the prince was often as obnoxious as he could be; he made life as difficult for the English tutor as possible. In despair at last, hardly knowing how to control his royal pupil, the Englishman had a purple rosette made, and the next morning at the appearance of the prince, he said, "I want to pin this in your coat." "What's that for?" "That is the royal color. It is not permitted me to punish you for any disobedience of the rules, but whenever you misbehave yourself, I am going to point at the purple." Then one day the prince acted in an ungentleman-like way; he was naughty. The tutor stopped, pointed to the purple, and immediately the prince colored and said, "I beg your pardon." It was the appeal to the purple, reminding the Dauphin that rank imposes obligation. God gives us an appeal — it is an appeal to the blue. We represent heaven. The world judges our Lord by us.

> "You are writing a Gospel, a chapter each day,
> By deeds that you do, by words that you say;
>
> Men read what you write, whether faithful or true —
> Say, what is the Gospel, according to you?"

16
After Death: What?
For the Christian

In attempting to answer this question concerning which there seems to be much perplexity in the minds of many sincere believers, it is hardly necessary to go outside of the fifth chapter of the second Epistle to the Corinthians, though one would include with this the last three verses of chapter 4, which properly belong to the chapter that follows. We will read from 4:16—5:10.

"For which cause we faint not; but though our outward man perish, yet the inward man is renewed day by day. For our light affliction, which is but for a moment, work-eth for us a far more exceeding and eternal weight of glory; While we look not at the things which are seen, but at the things which are not seen: for the things which are seen are temporal; but the things which are not seen are eternal.

For we know that if our earthly house of this tabernacle were dissolved, we have a building of God, a house not made with hands, eternal in the heavens. For in this we groan, earnestly desiring to be clothed upon with our house which is from heaven: If so be that being clothed we shall not be found naked. For we that are in this tabernacle do groan, being burdened; not for that we would be unclothed, but clothed upon, that mortality might be swallowed up of life. Now he that hath wrought us for the selfsame thing is God, who also hath given unto us the earnest of the Spirit.

Therefore we are always confident, knowing that, whilst we are at home in the body, we are absent from the Lord: (For we walk by faith, not by sight:) We are confident, I say, and willing rather to be absent from the body, and to be present with the Lord. Wherefore we labour, that, whether present or absent, we may be accepted of him. For we must all appear before the judgment seat of Christ; that every one may receive the things done in his body, according to that he hath done, whether it be good or bad."

You will notice that this passage abounds in striking contrasts. I want to point out a full dozen, or more of them; and doubtless a careful analysis would show several others, and some that I will mention could be subdivided, and thus add to the number.

First, we have the "outward man" contrasted with the "inward man." Notice this carefully. The outward man is the physical man; the inward man is the spiritual man. Materialists of all types deny the personality of the spiritual man, but verse 10 distinctly affirms it.

In the second place, "perish" is contrasted with "renewed." The physical man wastes away. As soon as we begin to live we begin to die; but the inward man is renewed from day to day.

Then in verse 17 we have three more decided contrasts: "light" is contrasted with "weight," "affliction" with "glory," and that "which is but for a moment" with that which is "eternal." Affliction often seems to the tried and distressed saint to be heavy indeed and long-continued, but the Spirit of God calls it "our light affliction, which is but for a moment," and we realize this in all its blessedness when we see it in full contrast with the "far more exceeding and eternal weight of glory," which is to be our portion throughout the ages to come.

The sixth contrast is in verse 18, where "the things which are seen" is put in apposition with "the things which are not seen." The former are declared to be temporal and the latter eternal. This sixth contrast is of great importance in connection with the present discussion. It is often said, by the advocates of conditional immortality and other materialistic systems, that the word generally rendered "eternal" in the New Testament does not necessarily bear that meaning. But here we have this very word put in direct contrast with the word "temporal." Temporal clearly means that which has an end. Eternal, therefore, must mean that which has no end. If we think of several other instances in which the same word is used we will perhaps realize more than ever the truthfulness and solemnity of this statement. We read of the eternal God, the eternal Spirit, eternal redemption, eternal inheritance; and on the other hand, of eternal punishment and eternal judgment. Who, with any regard for the authority of Scripture, would dare affirm that eternal means one thing when referred to what is good, and to Deity itself, but quite another when it has to do with the punishment of the wicked?

The seventh and eighth contrasts are found in the first verse of chapter 5. There we have "our earthly house of this tabernacle," and side by side with it, "a building of God, a house not made with hands, eternal in the heavens." The one may be "dissolved," the other is "eternal." Observe that this is the third time we have the word "eternal" used in this remarkable series: once more it is in direct contrast with that which passes away, or comes to an end; that which is temporal may be dissolved, but that which is eternal will never know dissolution.

We next have the contrast between being "un-clothed," which refers to death, and "clothed upon," which is clearly resurrection. Mortality will then be swallowed up of life.

The last three pairs of contrasts to which I now desire to direct your attention are found in verses 6 to 9, where we have, "at home in the body" in contrast with "absent from the body"; "by faith" contrasted with "by sight"; and, lastly, "absent from the Lord" contrasted with "pres-ent with the Lord."

I am persuaded that any thoughtful person, desiring to be taught of God, who will weigh carefully this full series of contrasts, will have no difficulty with regard to the future state of those who know the Lord Jesus Christ as their Saviour; but we will now proceed to look some-what carefully at the passage as a whole.

In the first place I call your attention again to the fact that we are not to confound the "outward" man with the "inward" man. I am not my body. Man is distinctly said to be spirit, and soul, and body. The body is the outward man. The spirit and the soul together constitute the inward man. The spirit is the seat of the intellectual being, a distinct entity, as we shall see when we come to consider this special topic in a separate lecture. The soul is the seat of the man's emotional nature. These two, spirit and soul, are never separated. Scripture alone distinguishes between them; that is, it shows us that they are distinct but it does not separate. Now all men, as created by God, consist of spirit, soul, and body; but the believer in the Lord Jesus Christ has that which the natural man does not possess. Being born again, he has received a new nature, and this new nature is also called "spirit"; it is the characteristic feature of the inward man. "That which is born of the flesh is flesh; and that which is born of the Spirit is spirit. Marvel not that I said unto them, Ye must be born again" (John 3:6, 7).

Unless it should be our happy lot to be among those who are still living in the body when the Lord Jesus Himself descends from heaven with that assembling shout spoken in I Thessalonians 4, we who believe in Him must go the way of all flesh. Our earthly house of this tabernacle must be dissolved — that is, the body will die. What then will be the state of the believer? When my body sleeps in death, do I, the inward man, go to sleep in the body? Or will I leave the body and ascend to another sphere?

Scripture gives no uncertain testimony in regard to this. The body is but the tabernacle in which the inward man dwells. The tabernacle may be broken down, and the man himself moves out. This is clearly what the apostle here teaches and it is confirmed by the words of his brother-apostle, Peter, in II Peter 1:13– 15. He there says, "Yea, I think it meet, as long as I am in this tabernacle, to stir you up by putting you in remembrance; Knowing that shortly I must put off this my tabernacle, even as our Lord Jesus Christ hath shewed me. Moreover I will endeavour that ye may be able after my decease to have these things always in remembrance."

Observe: while left on the earth he was in the tabernacle of his body; at death he put off his tabernacle. He speaks of this as his decease; this word here translated "decease" is the word "exodus"— the same as the title of the second book of the Bible. That book is called "Exodus" because it relates the going out of the people of Israel from the land of Egypt. Peter's exodus took place when the inward man moved out of the earthly tabernacle. And so with Paul; for in another very striking scripture (Phil. 1:21– 25) he tells us,

"For me to live is Christ, and to die is gain. But if I live in the flesh, this is the fruit of my labour: yet what I shall choose I wot not. For I am in a strait betwixt two, having a desire to depart, and to be with Christ; which is far better: Nevertheless to abide in the flesh is more needful for you. And having this confidence, I know that I shall abide and continue with you all for your further-ance and joy of faith."

Observe that here we have the same truth put in a slightly different way. Life here on earth is life in the flesh, that is, in the body; death is to "depart," that is, to go out, and to be with Christ which is far better. But for the then present time the apostle was convinced that he would still abide in the body. The great point is, the man himself is not confounded with his body. He is "far more than a living, breathing mass of clay," as one has well said; a veritable living spirit indwells this clay tene-ment for a brief period, moves out at death, but returns at the coming of the Lord Jesus Christ, when the body, raised in glory, and suited to heaven, becomes our soul's and spirit's eternal dwelling.

May I here use a very homely illustration? A number of years ago I was returning to my home-city from a gospel tour. My wife met me at the station, and as we came up through town on the way to our house I noticed that an entire block of stores had been vacated, as the whole building was being made over. Apparently an ar-rangement had been made with the tenants of all the stores to move out temporarily and return when the reno-vation was complete. In every window we noticed signs reading somewhat as follows: "Such and such a firm temporarily located at such a place, moved out until this building is renovated and repaired." I said to my wife, "What a striking picture of death for the believer! If I should be called home to be with the Lord before you, and you wished to put a slab of some kind where my body lies, you might have it read something like this: 'Henry A. Ironside, saved by the grace of God, moved out until renovated and repaired.' That would tell the whole story."

Months went by, and again I had been absent on a trip telling out the glad tidings of the grace of God, when upon my return I passed once more this same block of buildings. One would hardly have recognized it, so great was the change, and yet it was the same original foundation, the same walls and floors, but marvelously altered both within and without, and all the firms were back doing business at their old stands. I thought when I looked at it, What a picture of resurrection, when that which has been sown in weakness shall be raised in power, that which has been sown in dishonor shall be raised in glory, and the inward man shall dwell in the renewed body—identical with, yet different as to condition from the body that once wasted away.

I know the thought of some is that the building of God is a spirit-body of some kind which clothes the inward man between death and resurrection, but the verses which follow clearly negate this thought. In this present tabernacle we groan, earnestly desiring, not to die, but to be clothed upon with our house which is from heaven when we are caught up to meet the Lord in the air. Like Paul, we are set for the first resurrection, and if when raised or changed we are in Christ we shall not be found naked.

It is well to remember that resurrection does not necessarily involve salvation. There is to be "a resurrection both of the just and of the unjust"—a resurrection of life and a resurrection of damnation (John 5:29). There are those who in their resurrection body will be clothed in Christ's likeness, and those who in that day will be as they are now—poor and wretched, blind, miserable and naked.

But the fact that people are saved does not preclude them from groaning. We once groaned in anguish under the weight of our sins. From that groaning, thank God, the believer has been delivered; but we still groan and yearn for deliverance from the vicissitudes of this present life and from the conditions which so often hinder spiritual growth. We look for the redemption of the body— this body which so often hinders our spiritual aspirations. How many times we are made to realize that the spirit indeed is willing but the flesh is weak, and so we groan, desiring not that we be unclothed, but clothed with a body like that of our Lord. No right-minded Christian is yearning to die, for he should say with Paul, "For me to live is Christ"; but we do yearn for the glad hour when we shall be clothed upon; when mortality shall be swallowed up of life, when our bodies shall be conformed to His body of glory. Now we have eternal life in dying bodies; but in that blessed moment of our Lord's return, His quickening word will impart eternal life to our very bodies.

It is for this very thing that He has been working in us up to the present moment, and has given us His Spirit to dwell within us as earnest of the blessedness which shall be ours in that resurrection day. Meantime, though encompassed with infirmities, we have full confidence, knowing that while we are at home in the body we are absent from the Lord; whereas, if called to leave the body, we shall not go out to wander in space, nor sleep in unconsciousness, but shall at once be at home with the Lord. Walking, not by sight, but by faith grounded in the written Word, we have a confidence in view of death which enables us to say with Paul, "To depart and be with Christ is far better." "Therefore, we are willing to be absent from the body and to be present with the Lord."

Let no one rob you, dear believer, of the preciousness of those four words, "present with the Lord." A better rendering would be, "at home with the Lord." Now we are at home in the body and absent from the Lord, then we shall be absent from the body and at home with the Lord. When you think of the dear departed ones in Christ, comfort yourself with these heartening thoughts. They are at home. Oh, the sweetness of that word "home!" They were strangers and pilgrims here on earth; for His blessed name's sake they voluntarily relinquished the earthly claims. Now the wilderness journey, with all its trials for them, is in the past, and they rest at home. How could they enjoy this if in an unconscious condition between death and resurrection? If this cold thought were true, how could the apostle speak of being with Christ as "far better"? Surely he had not in view a sleep of unconsciousness.

It is true that in many places he does speak of death as a sleep; but mark, that which sleeps is that which is to be awakened. The body of the believer is put to sleep, and it will be awakened at the Lord's return. Notice what II Corinthians 4:14 says, "Knowing that he which raised up the Lord Jesus shall raise up us also by Jesus, and shall present us with you." This clearly is the body which is to be raised up by Jesus, even as God the Father raised the body of Jesus from death.

Again in I Thessalonians 4:13, 14 we read,

"But I would not have you to be ignorant, brethren, concerning them which are asleep, that ye sorrow not, even as others which have no hope. For if we believe that Jesus died and rose again, even so them also which sleep in Jesus will God bring with him."

The expression used in the fourteenth verse, "them also which sleep in Jesus" might be better translated "them also who have been put to sleep by Jesus"—just as a mother takes her tired, fretful, and suffering child, quietly soothing it to sleep, so the Lord Jesus puts His beloved people to sleep. By and by, when He returns from heaven, He will raise them up again. Then I Thessalonians 4:15–18 will be fulfilled.

> "For this we say unto you by the word of the Lord, that we which are alive and remain unto the coming of the Lord shall not prevent [or, precede] them which are asleep. For the Lord himself shall descend from heaven with a shout, with the voice of the archangel, and with the trump of God: and the dead in Christ shall rise first: Then we which are alive and remain shall be caught up together with them in the clouds, to meet the Lord in the air: and so shall we ever be with the Lord. Wherefore comfort one another with these words."

Some may ask, Do those who are absent from the body and at home with the Lord know anything of what goes on in this world? The best answer to that may be another question: What does Scripture say about it? And to this the answer would probably be, Nothing. Then, certainly, it is not wise for us to speculate. But is there *nothing* in Scripture which intimates that the redeemed in heaven have between death and resurrection at least *some* knowledge of things taking place on earth?

There is a passage in the beautiful fifteenth chapter of Luke which is most precious in this connection. There we read, in verse 7: "I say unto you, that even so there shall be joy in heaven over one sinner that repenteth, more than over ninety and nine righteous persons, which need no repentance." I quote from the Revised Version, and would lay special stress on the expression "even so."

The friends of the man who found the lost sheep were called upon by him to share his joy over its recovery. "Even so" are the friends of the Good Shepherd called upon to joy in *His* gladness over the salvation of a soul. In Luke 16 we see Abraham and the rich man in the full possession of their faculties, the one in paradise, the other in Hades. They are competent to enter into communications, the one with the other, though separated spiritually by a great gulf that can never be crossed. How much more will the redeemed in heaven hold communion with each other and with their Lord, and thus enter into His rejoicing when a sinner repents. It is not only angels who exult, but all in heaven.

At the close of a meeting some years ago a young man who had led a wild reckless life yielded to Christ. For over an hour several of us were seeking to help him from the Word of God. He was in great anguish of soul as he mourned over his past wickedness, and it was some time before he could see the simplicity of salvation through faith alone in Christ; but when at last he caught a view of that finished work, his soul entered into peace. With mingled tears of joy and grief running down his face he said to me, "Oh, if my dear mother were only living that I might send her a telegram tonight to let her know that I had yielded to Christ. She prayed for me for many years: my ungodliness broke her heart; she died praying that I might be saved. How glad I would be if I could only get word to her that at last her prayers were answered." I said, "My dear young man, you need not grieve over that. I am certain she knew the moment you trusted Christ. Up there in heaven every redeemed one is rejoicing over another sinner that repenteth."

And so we gather from these scriptures that there is no such thing as unconsciousness for the believer between death and resurrection; the moment that he leaves the body he is in the presence of the Lord, and waits there expectantly until the first resurrection at the Lord's return.

> "When the weary ones we love enter on their rest above,
> When their words of love and cheer fall no longer on
> our ear, Hush, be every murmur dumb! It is only 'till He
> come.' "

In that glad day the bodies of the sleeping saints will be awakened and the living will be changed in a moment. Then, throughout eternity, in bodies glorified, and wholly like the blessed Lord Himself, they will dwell in His presence, and be with Him in happiness unmarred and joy unclouded, in the home of the saints, the New Jerusalem.

For the Christless

Last evening I spoke to you on "After Death: What?—for *the Christian*." To-night my theme is a much more solemn and serious one: "After Death: What?—for *the Christless*." When we think of the realities of the life to come, it is as to the impenitent and the wicked that we are most exercised. We are not worried as to what the other world has in store for the men and women who have walked with God here. We feel certain, even apart from revelation, that wherever John, the beloved, will be for eternity, it must be well with him. We are sure that Paul, the devoted follower of his crucified and risen Master, cannot lose out in the coming ages as a result of his faithfulness here; nor are we concerned about repentant David, sinner though he owns himself to have been, or the dying robber, whose last words condemn himself and magnify his Saviour. With all these we are certain it must be well forever.

But we have deep exercise of heart when we think of Cain, who turned away from salvation purchased by atoning blood; of Esau, who sold his birthright for a mess of pottage; of Judas, the traitor, who bartered away his hope of everlasting bliss for thirty pieces of silver. When we think of these men and myriads like them, we ask with bated breath, What does the great eternal future hold in store for them?

In Job 14:10, we read, "man dieth, and wasteth away: yea, man giveth up the ghost, and where is he?" The old Anglo-Saxon word "ghost," similar to the German "geist," simply means "spirit." At death man gives up the spirit, and the question is, Where is he? The body may be buried or disposed of in some other way, but where is the spiritual entity, the man who at one time occupied that tenement? Notice another question in the fourteenth verse of the same chapter: "If a man die, shall he live again? all the days of my appointed time will I wait, till my change come."

There are then two questions: "Man dieth and wasteth away; man giveth up the spirit, and where is he?" Then, "If a man die, shall he live again?" The first question has to do with the state of the man between death and a possible resurrection; the last one inquires whether there will ever be a resurrection. Now in attempting to answer these questions from Scripture, remember we are confining ourselves to the Christless man. Where is he when the body dies, and will that body ever be raised from the tomb?

There is no authoritative answer to these questions apart from divine revelation. The speculations of men cannot give it, be they ever so reasonable and erudite. Those who reject the testimony of Holy Scripture are not further advanced in regard to the great question of life beyond the grave than that little coterie of Greek philosophers, who, in the days of Socrates, centuries before Christ, used to reason about life and death and immortality. Plato is still read and taught in our colleges. People still go back to those old Greeks for arguments regarding immortality; it is interesting, much that is advanced is fairly convincing and even probable, but there is no authoritative assurance; and the soul is left in uncertainty.

The Bible alone gives us positive knowledge. But to what part of our Bible shall we turn for light on these great questions? Not to the Old Testament. *Please keep that distinctly in mind.* There are those of a materialistic tendency, bearing a Christian name, but misguided people, as Adventists of various schools, Christadelphians, Russellites, and other minor sects, who insist that Scripture teaches the unconsciousness of the dead between death and resurrection, and in some instances the annihilation of the wicked after the day of judgment. Rarely indeed do these people quote from the New Testament in attempting to maintain their theories; they refer us almost invariably to Old Testament scriptures, and the bulk of these are found in three books, Job, the Psalms, and Ecclesiastes — particularly the latter.

Now we do well to remember that the Old Testament was not given to unfold the eternal future, but chiefly to show God's dealings with man, in this life, individually and nationally: and the three books mentioned are, of all others, the experimental books of the Old Testament, giving us human experience in striking detail.

It was our Lord Jesus Christ who brought life and immortality to light through the gospel.* Clearly then we need not expect to find these great truths fully developed in the Old Testament. There we have the twilight; in the later revelation we are in the full blaze of gospel light. I do not mean to say that saints of Old Testament times did not have the hope of immortality. They certainly did.

Job is perhaps the oldest book in the Bible, and unquestionably Job himself believed in a resurrection from the dead. He exclaims, "I know that my Redeemer liveth, and though after my skin worms destroy this body, yet in my flesh shall I see God." Moses speaks of the patriarchs as dying and going to be with their fathers, and Abraham could count on God to give him back Isaac from the dead if called upon to actually slay him on Mount Moriah. This, surely, he could not have done, had he not had the faith of immortality. David prayed and wept while his darling child was ill, but when he learned of his death he dried his eyes and comforted himself with the reflection, "He shall not come back to me, but I shall go to him," and elsewhere he exclaims, "I shall be satisfied when I awake in thy likeness."

I will not dwell upon the striking incident of Samuel's appearance to the witch of Endor, and his message to

---

*It is notable that the words "immortal," "immortality," and "eternal life" are not found in the Old Testament. They were as true then as now, of course, and *intuitively* believed in by the godly, but it awaited the coming of the Son of God for their open and full declaration. Atonement needed to be made before salvation could be openly preached in Christ's name, and the eternal issues revealed. — Ed.

Saul, "To-morrow shalt thou and thy sons be with me"; nor need I quote many passages in the Prophets which evince a knowledge of life after death. But, granting all these, it is certainly evident that it was not the specific purpose of any Old Testament writer to reveal this great truth, and in the experience books referred to, we need not be surprised if some passages even seem to indicate the contrary. These need to be carefully examined together with the context, that they be not entirely misapplied.

Here let me make a statement, seriously and soberly, which may startle some of you, and which you may even question at first. It is this: All the Bible is inspired, but there are many statements in it that are not true! Just think of it for a few moments—I want it to sink in. People often think that a text from any part of the Bible settles some controverted question, but a text out of its connection may be used to bolster up the worst kind of error; it may in fact be the declaration of an absolute falsehood.

We are told that some years ago a noted Southern attorney was pleading a certain case before a Kentucky jury where his client was on trial for his life. The prosecuting attorney, addressing the jury, said, "Gentlemen, we have it on the very highest authority that, 'All that a man hath will he give for his life.'" This made quite an impression on the jury, for they understood that he was quoting from the Bible—which he was. When he had concluded his address, the other attorney arose and said, "My opponent has told you that on the very highest authority we may know that all that a man hath will he give for his life." Then, opening a Bible, he read from the second chapter of the Book of Job how the devil said, "Skin for skin, yea, all that a man hath will he give for his life" (v. 4). "Now," he exclaimed dramatically, "Gentlemen of the jury, you know for yourselves who the attorney for the prosecution considers to be the very highest authority—even the devil himself!"

True, that statement is in the Bible; Satan made it, and it is only too true with many. But it is not invariably true that "all that a man hath will he give for his life." Myriads of our Lord's devoted followers have imitated their Master in laying down their lives rather than surrender one jot or tittle of the truth of God.

The above mentioned incident will show you what I mean when I say there are things related in the Bible which are not true. Not only are there statements in the Bible which are said to be from the devil himself, but there are some things spoken by good men, such as the friends of Job, for instance, who were not inspired of the Holy Spirit to speak as they did. There are statements uttered by very bad men recorded in the volume of inspiration, which do not thereby become divine truth. Thoughts and reasonings of the natural man's mind are sometimes given, as in the Book of Ecclesiastes. It is very important to bear this in mind when reading the experience books of the Old Testament.

In the Book of Ecclesiastes, Solomon tells us that they who have died will never any more have a reward. If we take that at its face value it would directly contradict New Testament revelation, as well as Solomon's own declaration by divine inspiration at the end of the book where he says,

"Let us hear the conclusion of the whole matter: Fear God, and keep his commandments: for this is the whole duty of man. For God shall bring every work into judgment, with every secret thing, whether it be good, or whether it be evil" (12:13, 14).

Is it an evidence of the non-inspiration of the Book of Ecclesiastes? Surely not. What then? In this book Solomon tells us he is giving us a record of what he said in his heart as he pondered things under the sun. He saw people die, they were buried, he never saw them come back from the tomb. We read elsewhere, "The dead know not anything." Does this mean they are absolutely unconscious after leaving the body? Not at all. Scripture elsewhere contradicts such a thought; but a lifeless corpse knows nothing of the affairs that occupied that busy brain but yesterday.

Shallow thinkers take such a passage as this, "The dead know not anything," and in the face of all the New Testament teachings to the contrary, deduce from it the doctrine of the "sleep of the soul." But the expression means nothing of the kind. The same words are used in that incident told in the first Book of Samuel, of the compact between David and Jonathan. David was hiding in the field; Jonathan had gone in to sound his father and find out whether David's life was really in danger. It had been agreed that Jonathan accompanied by a lad would go out into the field and shoot an arrow; if he said to the lad, "The arrow is beyond you," David would understand Saul was seeking his life; but if he said, "The arrow is behind you," he knew he was safe. The program was carried out, and Jonathan called to the lad, "The arrow is beyond you," and David understood; but we read that "the lad knew not anything." Was the boy in a state of unconsciousness? Not at all, but he knew nothing of the compact made between David and Jonathan. Time forbids calling your attention to a number of similar instances where exactly the same expression is used. You can look them up for yourself at your leisure.

In the last chapter of the Book of Malachi there is a

passage which many seem to think settles the question as to the fate of the wicked dead. I read verses 1 to 3:

> "For, behold, the day cometh that shall burn as an oven; and all the proud, yea, and all that do wickedly, shall be stubble: and the day that cometh shall burn them up, saith the LORD of hosts, that it shall leave them neither root nor branch. But unto you that fear my name shall the Sun of righteousness arise with healing in his wings; and ye shall go forth, and grow up as calves of the stall. And ye shall tread down the wicked; for they shall be ashes under the soles of your feet in the day that I shall do this, saith the LORD of hosts."

Now observe what the prophet is here telling Israel. Is he speaking of judgment to come on the wicked after death? Not at all. The passage is prophetic of what shall befall the wicked on the earth at the Lord's second coming. In other words, this judgment is pre-millennial, not post-millennial. There is nothing here about the resurrection and people brought before the Great White Throne. The day that "shall burn as an oven" is the day of the Lord, when wicked men, taken red-handed in their sins, will be burned up root and branch; that is, root and fruits. Then the righteous shall tread down the wicked. They shall be ashes under their feet in the day that God shall do this.

Does this prove the annihilation of those who die in their sins? No, it is similar in character to the judgment that fell on Sodom and Gomorrah. The day that Lot and his company left the city the fire of God's wrath burned up the people of the cities of the plains, root and branch. Had Lot himself and Abraham, his uncle, gone down to see conditions a few days after the judgment, the wicked would have been ashes under the soles of their feet; but does that imply annihilation? No. In the Book of Jude, written centuries after, we read of "Sodom and Gomorrah, and the cities about them ... set forth for an example, suffering the vengence of eternal fire" (v. 7). And our Lord Jesus Christ declares that "it shall be more tolerable for Sodom and Gomorrah in the day of judgment" than for those who rejected His word while He spake on earth. So, although burned up root and branch, although as ashes under the feet of the righteous, the people of Sodom and Gomorrah have not lost their identity; they are consciously suffering now, and will rise in the day of judgment.

Time forbids dwelling longer on the Old Testament, and I turn at once to the words of our Lord Jesus Christ Himself, rather than to those of His apostles. Not that I place the teaching of the Lord Jesus on a higher plane than that of His inspired apostles, but because many say, "I am not prepared to accept Paul, Peter, or John, but give me what Jesus says." So I shall do this. Men who reject the solemn warnings given elsewhere in the Bible as to the eternal judgment of the wicked, foolishly say that the teaching of Jesus is all they want—the Sermon on the Mount is enough for them.

Well, my friends, do you know that eternal punishment is taught in the Sermon on the Mount? And if you tell me that you will accept the teachings of Jesus Christ, don't forget that He has told us more of the actual state of the Christless dead than any one else. No one ever uttered more serious and solemn things as to the doom awaiting sinners than God's blessed Son, the tenderest, yet most faithful Man that ever walked this earth. It was not Peter who first spoke of "the fire that never shall be quenched"; it was not Paul who spoke of being "salted with fire"; it was not John who said, "It is better to enter into life maimed than having two hands to be cast into hell fire"; *it was the Lord Jesus Christ Himself;* and whatever further instruction you get in the New Testament in regard to the punishment of the wicked is all based on the teaching of the Son of God.

We have this teaching in its simplest and clearest form in the sixteenth chapter of Luke's Gospel. I know that some object, "Oh, that is only a parable." Who told you so? It is not called a parable. A parable is an illustration, or story, told to picture some truth. This incident of the rich man and Lazarus is not called a parable. The parables are generally announced by some such expression as this, "He spake a parable unto them," but we have no such expression here. But in the second place, if this is a parable it certainly is meant to illustrate the fearful danger of dying unreconciled to God; and the impression made on the minds of His hearers, and on those of millions of people from that day to this, is that Jesus was here teaching that it is a fearful thing to die in one's sins.

But notice the naturalness with which the story is introduced. Our Lord is addressing the people; and in the course of His instruction He says in the most natural way, "There was a certain rich man, which was clothed in purple and fine linen, and fared sumptuously every day" (v. 19). "There was a certain rich man"; was there, or was there not? Jesus says there was. He does not say, "Let us suppose there might have been such a person," but He definitely declares there was such a man; how he was clothed; how he fed sumptuously. Suppose in the course of my address I should say there was a certain Indian out in Arizona who was recently converted. When I get through you come up to me and say, "I was interested in what you told us about that Indian. How long ago was he converted?" "Oh," I say, "I hope you did not take me seriously, that was just a parable. I was only illustrating; I don't know of any such Indian." You would be justified in saying to me, "That, sir, was dishonest of you; you gave us all the distinct impression that you knew just such a person."

Now this is exactly what Jesus did. He gave every hearer that day to believe that He was relating a story of fact. When He comes to speak of the other man in the story, He says, "There was a certain beggar named Lazarus." When you are just supposing an incident to illustrate a point you don't usually name the suppositious character. Why did He name this beggar? Because He knew him: "He calleth his own sheep by name." We shall never know the rich man's name until the day of judgment, but we do know the beggar's name, because though poor in purse he was rich in faith, and was one of the sheep of Christ. Our Lord relates the story with remarkable detail, even to the dogs who came and licked the poor man's sores. If this is but a parable, what are these parabolic dogs who licked the parabolic sores of the parabolic beggar as he lay on the parabolic steps of the parabolic rich man's parabolic house, watching him eat his parabolic food? Often had the hearers of Jesus seen just such an incident as he was describing. He goes on to say that the beggar died and was carried by the angels into Abraham's bosom. This, of course, was before the death and resurrecton of our Lord Jesus Christ. Abraham was the father of the faithful, and in paradise. As a son of Abraham, this redeemed beggar was welcomed to his bosom. Believers now are said at death to be "absent from the body and present with the Lord." To be in Abraham's bosom was the portion of Old Testament saints.

And what about the rich man? He also died and was buried, and we follow his disembodied spirit into the other world. Jesus said, "In hell he lifted up his eyes, being in torment." Now, my friends, there have been times when I would have taken that out of the Bible if I could, and even tonight I can well understand the feelings of Richard Baxter as he prayed, "Oh, for a full heaven and an empty hell!" I have searched this book, and read scores of volumes penned by theologians of all shades of opinion, to try and find one ray of hope for men who died in their sins, but I have never been able to find it.

Men try to take the edge off a passage like this by setting aside the old Anglo-Saxon word "hell" and using the Greek word "Hades." We are told that this word has no reference whatever to a place of punishment; Hades is simply "the unseen." Very well, let us use the Greek word: "In Hades he lifted up his eyes, being in torment." Changing the name of the place, you see, does not do away with the torment.

But others say, "You are mistaken when you think of Hades as a condition in which men are found after death. Hades is simply the grave." I do not believe this for one moment. Scripture, I am certain, teaches the very opposite. But suppose, for argument's sake, we substitute the word "grave" for "hell." Let us read it that way: "In the grave he lifted up his eyes, being in torment." Again the change of the word fails to do away with the torment. You may call it the tomb; you may designate it simply the "unseen"; you may make it read the "spirit-world"; you may use any term you like, but the solemn fact remains that wherever that rich man was, and whatever that word means, he was *in torment!*

Need we follow the story further? Need we dwell upon its horrors? You know them well. You know how this wretched man, lost beyond redemption, becomes a suppliant in the pit of woe. He makes two agonized petitions, but they are denied him. He began to pray on the wrong side of death. He prays first for one drop of water on the tip of the beggar's finger to cool his parched tongue. Living water he had refused while grace was free, now he is where living water never flows through all eternity. His other request is for his five brothers. People say, "If I am lost I shall be with the crowd anyway. I shall have lots of company in hell." But, my friends, look at this—six brothers, but what a family! One is in hell and five are on the way; and the man in hell prays, "If you can do anything to keep my brothers from joining me here, do it; I don't want their company; send Lazarus that he may warn them and tell them not to come to this place of torment." Abraham replies, "They have Moses and the prophets; let them hear them." That is, they have the Bible—just what you have, and which you are responsible to heed. The man in torment cries, "No, father Abraham, but if one went unto them from the dead they would repent." Abraham answers, "If they hear not Moses and the prophets, neither will they be persuaded though one rose from the dead." Accept the testimony of this Book, receive the Saviour it reveals, or go into the outer darkness forever! There is no other alternative. It must be Christ or hell, and to reject the one is to choose the other.

But we must not ignore the attempt to make this incident a parable. If it is a parable, what is it supposed to teach? One, whose propaganda has misled thousands in recent years undertakes to explain it. He says the rich man is the Jew, the poor man is the Gentile. For centuries the Jew had all the good things; the favor of God, riches spiritual and material; he fared sumptuously every day; the Gentile lay outside this his door, afflicted, destitute, desiring to be fed with the crumbs which fell from the Jew's table. Eventually things changed; both Jew and Gentile died to their former condition. Now the Gentile has been brought into Abraham's bosom, the blessings that once belonged to the Jew are his, and the Jew is being tormented in Russia, in Poland, and in many parts of the world, where he is in agony. And the distressed Jew, from his place of torment, pleads for mercy. He says, Send the friends with some little message from the Word of God; relieve my agony, or deliver my brethren. But Abraham replies, "Between us and you there is a great gulf fixed, you cannot come to where the Gentile is, and the Gentile cannot come to you." Does this explain the so-called parable? Why, my friends, it does not fit! The gulf is not fixed between Jew and Gentile. Any Jew who will may enter into the fulness of Christian privilege, and any Gentile, who is foolish enough to do so, may apostatize and go over to Jewish ground.

But, you say, according to your understanding of the passage the man there is in torment before the day of judgment. If this be so, what need of a day of judgment?

Let me use a very simple illustration. A man is arrested, charged with a heinous crime. He is placed under restraint in the county jail; there he remains for long, weary months, and, if actually guilty, is tormented with a hidden knowledge of his guilt, however vehemently he may deny it, until at last he is brought to trial, and if the case goes against him he is sent to the penitentiary. Hades is God's jail; Gehenna is God's penitentiary.

In the twentith chapter of Revelation we read of a time when death and Hades will give up the dead which are in them. Death gives up the body, Hades gives up the spirit and soul. This is the resurrection of judgment, and it takes place a thousand years later than the resurrection of life. John writes,

"And I saw a great white throne, and him that sat on it, from whose face the earth and the heaven fled away; and there was found no place for them. And I saw the dead, small and great, stand before God; and the books were opened: and another book was opened, which is the book of life: and the dead were judged out of those things which were written in the books, according to their works. And the sea gave up the dead which were in it; and death and hell delivered up the dead which were in them: and they were judged every man according to their works. And death and hell were cast into the lake of fire. This is the second death. And whosoever was not found written in the book of life was cast into the lake of fire" (vv. 11–15).

This is the last great assize. Then men will be judged, every man according to his works, and punishment will be meted out in intrinsic righteousness. Who can tell all that is involved in the horror expressed by the symbol, "the lake of fire!" Oh, my friend, I pray you, run not the risk of finding out for yourself, but flee at once to Christ for refuge, and be able to say with Paul Gerhardt,

"There is no condemnation, there is no hell for me,
The torment and the fire mine eyes shall never see."

Actual details of the sinner's final doom are not given, but striking and awful figures are used, such as "wandering stars to whom is reserved the blackness of darkness forever"; "beaten with stripes," "cast into a furnace of fire," and many others. These all are meant to impress men with the fearfulness of an eternity away from God — an eternity out of Christ! Risk not, I pray you, so dire a doom, but flee now for refuge to Him who waits in grace to save.

Spirit and Soul and Body

> "I pray God your whole spirit and
> soul and body be preserved blameless
> unto the coming of our Lord Jesus"
> (I Thess. 5:23).

Because God has existed from all eternity as one ineffable Being in three glorious Persons, the Father, the Son and the Holy Spirit — all co-equal in majesty, power, and all attributes — we speak of Him as "the Trinity." The word itself is not found in the pages of Holy Scripture, but the fact is again and again declared, and perhaps nowhere more strikingly than in the formula of Christian baptism: "Baptizing them unto the Name of the Father, and the Son, and the Holy Spirit." Observe, not the names, as though they were three Beings, but the Name — the three are one.

Because man was created as one person in three parts we speak of him as tri-partite. He is spirit and soul and body. The body alone is not man; the soul alone is not man; the spirit alone is not man; but spirit and soul and body together constitute man. It is my purpose on this occasion to inquire what Scripture teaches as to the meaning of these terms.

It is hardly necessary to say much about the body; that is the material part of man, and is his link with the material creation as a whole. The body is the house in which the inward man dwells. In its present condition it is subject to decay and death; but there will be a resurrection of both the just and the unjust, when the bodies of the saved and the lost will be raised from the dead. In their resurrected material bodies the saints will stand at the judgment seat of Christ to be rewarded according to the deeds done in the body; and the wicked, raised a thousand years later, will stand at the Great White Throne to be judged according to their deeds.

It may be well to turn back to the first page of our Bibles and notice how in the beginning we have a three-fold creation: that is, three times in this wonderful first chapter of Genesis God is said to have "created." In verse one we read, "God created the heaven and the earth." Here you have the origin of *matter*. We never read of a second creation of anything material. All the matter in the universe is formed out of that which was then created.

In verse 21 we have a *second* creative act: "God created great whales, and every living creature that moveth"; or as better rendered, "Every being that hath *a living soul*." Here is the origin of life. Scripture knows nothing of life spontaneously generated from dead matter. It differentiates absolutely between the non-living and the living. By no possible process of evolution could the non-living ever become the living. Therefore, if dependent life is to come into the universe, God must act anew as Creator.

Soul, as we shall see, is that which is common both to the lower animals and to man. It is the natural life with all its capabilities of passions, emotions and instincts. The soul of the animal dies when the body dies; with the soul of man it is otherwise, being linked with his spirit.

I remember some years ago I was in the town of Los Gatos in California, having a series of meetings. A Seventh-day Adventist was lecturing there at the same time, in a large tent. As I passed the tent one day I noticed a very imposing sign on one side. In large letters I read:

TEN THOUSAND DOLLARS REWARD

"I will give $10,000.00 United States Gold Coin, to any one who will produce a text from the Bible that speaks of an immortal soul."

I went inside to find the lecturer. He was there dusting the seats. I said, "I have come to see you, sir, about the sign outside." "Oh," he replied, agreeably enough, "you have come to collect the $10,000; have you?" "No," I answered, "I am afraid I cannot claim it on your terms." "You admit then," he replied, "that the Bible nowhere speaks of an immortal soul." I acknowledged this without hesitation. Then I asked, "Because the Bible nowhere speaks of an immortal soul, do you therefore believe that the soul of man is mortal?" "Certainly," he answered; "undoubtedly if the Bible never speaks of an immortal soul, the soul must be mortal."

I drew his attention to the fact that just as the Bible does not mention an immortal soul, neither does it ever speak of a mortal soul. I pointed out that, arguing from his standpoint, it was just as reasonable to say that the soul of man is not mortal, since the Bible never mentions a mortal soul. But I went on, "If I can produce a scripture that declares the soul is not killed when the body is killed, will you give me the $10,000? For, I suppose, by an immortal soul you mean a soul that lives when the body dies."

He at once began to hedge, and said, "It might be a question of interpretation," and I saw that my chances of earning the $10,000 were exceedingly slim. However, I produced the passage. You will find it in Matthew 10:28.

There our Lord says, "Fear not them which kill the body, but are not able to kill the soul." Manifestly, a soul that cannot be killed when the body is killed must be what we mean when we speak of "an immortal soul." The Adventist was taken aback for the moment, but though silenced, refused to part with the $10,000. The fact is that in Scripture the actual words, "mortal" and "immortal," are only used in reference to the body. The mortal body becomes immortal if the believer lives on earth until the return of the Lord from heaven.

Turning again to Genesis 1, we have a *third* act of creation. In verse 27 we read: "So God created man in his own image, in the image of God created he him." Why the need of this distinctive creative act if man is simply an evolution from the animals beneath him? The fact is that by no possibility could creatures possessing only body and soul have become possessed of a thinking, reasoning spirit, unless it were communicated by God Himself. It is this that lifts man above all else in God's creation. If you turn to Zechariah 12:1, you will read, "The burden of the word of the *Lord* for Israel, saith the *Lord,* which stretcheth forth the heavens, and layeth the foundation of the earth, and formeth the spirit of man within him." Observe that the formation of the human spirit is there viewed as though it were as great a work as the stretching forth of the heavens and the creation of the earth. Does not this give us some idea of its importance in the mind of God?

Now just what is the spirit in man? Perhaps the clearest passage in the Bible is found in I Corinthians 2:11: "For what man knoweth the things of a man, save the spirit of the man which is in him? even so the things of God knoweth no man, but the Spirit of God." Here the spirit of man is shown to be the seat of intelligence. It is by the spirit man knows; it is the spirit that reasons. It is the spirit that receives instruction from God. Several other scriptures will help to make this clear. Romans 8:16: "The Spirit itself beareth witness with our spirit, that we are the children of God." Romans 1:9: "God is my witness, whom I serve with my spirit in the gospel of his Son." Job 32:8: "There is a spirit in man; and the inspiration of the Almighty giveth them understanding." Notice that understanding is received by the spirit through divine inspiration. Proverbs 18:14: "The spirit of a man will sustain his infirmity; but a wounded spirit who can bear?" 20:27: "The spirit of man is the candle of the LORD, searching all the inward parts of the belly"; that is, illuminating the man's inward being. God illuminates the man by communicating His truth to the spirit. We might quote many other scriptures, but these will suffice as they clearly emphasize the case in point. It is the spirit that thinks; it is the spirit that weighs evidence; the spirit is the part of the man to which God, who is Himself a Spirit, communicates His mind.

At death the spirit leaves the body. This, in fact, is what death is—the separation of body and spirit. In James 2:26 we are told, "as the body without the spirit is dead, so faith without works is dead also."

We have already seen that when the body of the beast dies, the soul, which is linked with its body, dies too; that is the end of its existence. But when the body of the man dies, his spirit leaves the body, whether the person is saved or unsaved. "Then shall the dust return to the earth as it was: and the spirit return to God who gave it" (Eccles. 12:7). Leaving the earthly tenement behind, the spirit goes into the unseen world and has to do with the God who created it. This is alike true of the saved and the lost. Both have to give account to God.

Materialists insist that the spirit is but the breath; they point to the fact that in both the Hebrew and the Greek languages the words for "breath," "wind," and "spirit" are the same, and they insist that therefore in each instance the word may be translated "breath" with impunity. However, it is well for us to remember that even in English the word "spirit" has a number of meanings, according to the connection in which it is used, and these meanings cannot be confounded without doing violence to the language. We speak of a man of spirit, and we mean of decision of purpose and of energy. We speak of a spirit, and we mean a wraith or a ghost. The context determines the meaning of the word. The best way to find out whether the spirit of man is simply the breath of the man is to try translating for ourselves. Substitute the word "breath" in the various passages we have already quoted, and see if it fits. "I pray God that your *breath* ... be preserved blameless" (I Thess. 5:23) — will that do? We all agree that a blameless breath is desirable, but can any one think the apostle speaks of such a thing here? Again, "What man knoweth the things of a man save the breath of a man that is in him?" Whoever heard of an intelligent breath? Nor is it the "breath" of the man that is the candle of the Lord; neither does the Spirit of God bear witness with our "breath" that we are children of God, and Paul's service in the gospel was far more than service with his "breath." I do not want to amuse nor try to be humorous, but it is necessary sometimes to show how ridiculous such fantastic theories are, to show that they refute themselves.

What then shall we say of the *soul* in man? That it is not to be confounded with the spirit, our opening text makes plain. The use of the copulative "and" between spirit and soul emphasizes this. In Hebrews 4:12 we read:

"The word of God is quick, and powerful, and sharper than any two-edged sword, piercing even to the dividing asunder of soul and spirit, and of the joints and marrow, and is a discerner of the thoughts and intents of the heart."

Here we learn that God's Word distinguishes between soul and spirit. It does not separate them, for the two are never separated, either in life or in death. The spirit is the higher part of the unseen man: that part, as we have already seen, to which the Spirit of God speaks. The soul is the lower part of the unseen man, and is the link between the body and the spirit. It is not merely the natural life, though it is that, but it is a great deal more. It is the seat of man's emotional nature.

Again let me give a number of quotations from Scripture. First, one that speaks of God having a soul. "Now the just shall live by faith: but if any man draw back, my soul shall have no pleasure in him" (Heb. 10:38). And in the next verse we read, "But we are not of them that draw back unto perdition; but of them that believe to the saving of the soul." God's soul longs for the salvation of our souls; that is, God, who is infinite love, would have our emotional natures in fullest harmony with His own. Hindrances to this are found in our bodily lusts. I Peter 2:11: "Abstain from fleshly lusts, which war against the soul." The soul in harmony with God finds its joys in Him, and in this the spirit fully shares. Luke 1:46: "And Mary said, My soul doth magnify the Lord, And my spirit hath rejoiced in God my Saviour."

The soul *suffers*. Luke 2:35: "A sword shall pierce through thy own soul also." Psalm 107:26: "Their soul is melted because of trouble." Joseph's brethren "saw the anguish of his soul," but took no heed. Jesus said, "Now is my soul troubled," and in His agony on the cross, "His soul was made an offering for sin"; yea, there,

"He poured out his soul unto death," when "he was numbered with the transgressors." See Isaiah 53:12.

The soul *loves.* "Saw you him whom my soul loveth?" exclaims the bride in the Canticles. In I Samuel 18:1, "The soul of Jonathan was knit with the soul of David, and Jonathan *loved* him as his own soul."

The soul *hates.* II Samuel 5:8: "The lame and the blind, that are hated of David's soul."

The soul *mourns.* Job 14:22: "His soul within him shall mourn."

The soul *desires.* Job 23:13: "What his soul desireth, even that he doeth."

The soul *longs.* Psalm 119:20: "My soul breaketh for the longing that it hath unto thy judgments at all times." Psalm 42:1, 2: "As the hart panteth after the water brooks, so panteth my soul after thee, O God. My soul thirsteth for God." Psalm 63:1: "My soul thirsteth for thee."

These are but a very few out of many similar scriptures that we might quote did time permit, but they surely establish the fact that the soul is the seat of the emotional nature just as the spirit is the seat of the intellectual nature; and because man in the present body is so largely a creature of emotions, the soul is made to designate the man as a whole. Man is distinctly called a soul over and over again. "Man became a living soul" (Gen. 2:7). And in Luke 12:20 the Lord says to the rich fool, "This night thy soul shall be required of thee." Whereas, in Revelation 6, John sees in a vision the souls under the altar of those who have been slain. It is altogether correct, therefore, to speak of man as having a soul to be saved or a soul to be lost.

Someone has likened man as originally created by God to a three-story house; the lower story or basement is the body; the second story, or workshop, is the soul; the third story, as the observatory and the place of communion and study, is the spirit. In his sinless condition, man's spirit held converse with God and enjoyed communion with the Infinite Spirit. The fall of man, as a moral earthquake, so shook the house that the third story fell down into the basement. The natural man is therefore the soulish man. The word rendered "natural" and "sensual" in the New Testament, is really "soulish." It is an adjective derived from the word for soul.

Man, however, is not bereft of the spirit even though fallen, but he has "the understanding darkened, being alienated from the life of God, through the ignorance which is in him." No act on man's part can ever restore the spirit to its proper place, for all his faculties have been perverted by the fall. His spirit has become insubject to God, and made filthy by sin. We read, you remember, of the "filthiness of the flesh and spirit." His soul has become utterly debased and corrupt; he now loves what God hates, and hates what God loves. His body is weakened by disease and infirmity, the direct result of the entrance of sin into the world. He is gone out of the way, and is become altogether unprofitable. In other words, man is a hopelessly ruined creature, apart from the regenerating grace of God.

But it is the mind of God to save this fallen, debased man; and not only to restore him to his Adamic condition, but to lift him to a higher plane than unfallen man ever knew. In order that this might be so, God, Himself, in the person of the Son, came into this scene as man. He not only took a human body, but was possessed of a true human spirit and human soul. Many do not see this, and think of the divine *Logos,* the Eternal Word, bearing the same relation to His body as our spirit and soul do to our body—which is a mistake. Christ not only took a body as a tabernacle for Deity, but He took a complete humanity into union with Deity, thus becoming manifested on earth as the Son of God — a Being with two natures, human and divine.

That He had a human soul is clear from the passages already quoted. In another place He says, "My soul is exceedingly sorrowful, even unto death." It is written also that, "He was troubled in his spirit"; "He rejoiced in spirit"; and as He was about to lay down His life, He exclaimed, "Father, into thy hands I commend my spirit." He offered Himself a sacrifice in full — body, soul, and spirit on behalf on our ruined humanity.

The atoning blood that purchases redemption was a man's blood untainted by sin. The body given on the cross was a human body holy and undefiled. The anguish of His soul was the anguish of a human soul, which we can but faintly enter into as He suffered there in the deepest recesses of His being; all His tenderest affections were lacerated as He took our place in judgment upon the cross. The darkness that overwhelmed His spirit we can but faintly apprehend as we listen to His fearful cry, "My God, my God, why hast thou forsaken me?" His was a complete sacrifice of Himself on our behalf.

When a soul trusts Him as Saviour, a new life is communicated to the man once wrecked and ruined, and this life is felt — shall I say? — in every part. The awakened spirit now receives the word of God, and the man is renewed in the spirit of his mind; the building is being renewed so that once more he is able to look up to God and enter into communion with Him through the spirit — is able to take in and understand the mind of God, and to discern what is according to the Word. His soul also is saved; its affections are purified; its longings and yearnings are now turned from things evil and things mundane to things holy and heavenly.

The body alone remains for the present unchanged, save as the new life enables the man to resist physical appetites that once threatened to ruin this tabernacle, now recognized as the temple of the living God; but eventually, at the coming of the Lord Jesus Christ, He will change this body of our humiliation and make it like unto the body of His glory. Then we shall be completely saved—spirit, soul, and body. We shall then have put off the natural body and have put on a spiritual body.

Some, however, when reading I Corinthians 15:44, mentally contrast, I think, a material body with an immaterial one. But this is not the thought of the apostle nor the mind of the Spirit. A natural body is a body suited to the soul; the word rendered "natural" is simply, as already mentioned, an adjective derived from the word for "soul." We might say a soulish body. It is raised a spiritual body—not a body of spirit, but a real body suited to the spirit. Now the spirit often is willing, but the flesh is weak; then body and spirit will be in perfect harmony. This will be our complete salvation, when spirit, soul, and body will be conformed to the image of our Lord Jesus Christ, the Firstborn among many brethren.

> "When left this scene of fault and strife
>   Then flesh and sense deceive no more.
> We then shall see the Prince of life
>   And all His ways of grace explore."

We shall be wholly like Him, and His suited companions, in glorified bodies like His own, forever. "Faithful is he that calleth you, who also will do it." For it is written, "He who hath began a good work in you will perform it until the day of Jesus Christ." In that day our salvation will be complete, when our entire spirit and soul and body will be blameless before God, as we stand in His presence in all the perfection of Christ's finished work.

Excerpts from

Illustrations Of Bible Truths

Excerpt from the Preface

I think it was Charles H. Spurgeon who said, "The sermon is the house; the illustrations are the windows that let in the light." *But most minds are so constituted that they need illustrations to enable them readily to grasp the full import of the message.*

17
Doubtful Things

"He that doubteth is condemned if he eat" (Rom. 14:23, R.V.).

Sandy was a thrifty Scot who objected to needless laundry expense, so when he wore a dress shirt to a banquet, he put it away carefully for future use. On one occasion when dressing for such an event, he took a used shirt out of the drawer and examined it with care, hoping to be able to wear it that evening. Not being quite sure of its strict cleanliness, he took it to a window, where he was looking it over under a better light than the room afforded. His wife, Jean, noticed him shaking his head as though fearful that it would not pass careful scrutiny.

"Remember, Sandy," she called to him, "if it's doubtful, it's dirty."

That settled it. The shirt went into the discard and another—a fresh one—took its place. Jean's words may well speak to every believer concerning things about which conscience raises any question whatsoever.

18
Lost in the Church

"If our gospel be hid, it is hid to them
that are lost" (II Cor. 4:3).

In an English village a Sunday school entertainment was being held in a small church. The place was crowded and in darkness as a stereopticon exhibition was being given. A knock at the door summoned an usher, who made his way to the front and announced, "Little Mary Jones is lost. Her family and the town officers have been searching everywhere for her. If anyone has seen her or knows of her whereabouts, will he please go to the door and communicate with the friend who is inquiring." No one moved and the lecturer went on with his address and pictures.

At the close, when the lights were turned on, a lady noticed Mary sitting on a front seat. Going over to her, she said,

"Why, Mary, didn't you hear them inquiring for you? Why did you not let them know you were here?"

Surprised, the child asked, "Did they mean me? They said Mary Jones was lost. I am not lost. I knew where

I was all the time; I thought it was some other Mary Jones."

She was lost in the church and did not know it. How many others are like her. They have a name that they live, but are dead. Though members of some local church, they have never seen their need of Christ, nor have they believed the message of the gospel.

19
Encouragement to Pray

"And all things, whatsoever ye shall
ask in prayer, believing, ye shall
receive" (Matt. 21:22).

A number of years ago it was my privilege to
attend a Bible conference at which the late Dr. D. M.
Stearns was the main speaker. On one particular occasion he had a question hour, and, among the questions
there was one that I never forgot. It read something like
this: "If you had prayed all your life for the salvation of
a loved one, and then you got word that that person had
died without giving any evidence of repentance after having lived a sinful life, what would you think, both of
prayer itself and of the love of God and His promises to
answer?"

It was a very striking question and I know that everyone in the room sat up and wondered what the doctor
would have to say in reply to it.

He said, "Well, dear sister, I should expect to meet

that loved one in heaven, for I believe in a God who answers prayer, and if He put that exercise upon your heart to pray for that dear one, it was because He, doubtless, intended to answer it."

Then he told a story. Many years ago there was a dear old lady living in Philadelphia who had a very wayward son. This young man had been brought up in church and Sunday school, but he had drifted away from everything holy. He had gone to sea and had become a very rough, careless, godless sailor.

One night his mother was awakened with a very deep sense of need upon her heart. When fully awake, she thought of her son and she was impressed that he was in great danger; as a result, she got up, threw on a dressing gown, knelt by her bedside, and prayed earnestly that God would undertake for the boy, whatever his need was. She didn't understand it, but after praying for perhaps two or three hours there came to her a sense of rest and peace, and she felt sure in her heart that God had answered. She got back into bed and slept soundly until the morning. Day after day she kept wondering to herself why she was thus awakened and moved to prayer, but somehow or other she could not feel the need to pray for that boy any more; rather she praised God for something which she felt He had done for her son.

Several weeks passed. One day there was a knock at the door. When she went to the door — there stood her boy! As soon as he entered the room, he said, "Mother, I'm saved!" Then he told her a wonderful story.

He told how a few weeks earlier, his ship had been tossed in mid-Atlantic by a terrific storm; and it looked as though there were no hope of riding it through. One of the masts had snapped; the captain called the men to come and cut it away. They stepped out, he among them, cursing and reviling God because they had to be out in such an awful night. They were cutting away this mast when suddenly the ship gave a lurch, and a great wave caught this young man and carried him overboard.

As he struggled almost helplessly with the great waves of the sea, the awful thought came to him, "I'm lost forever!" Suddenly, he remembered a hymn that he had often heard sung in his boyhood days, "There is life in a look at the crucified One; There is life at this moment for thee; Then look, sinner, look unto Him and be saved; Unto Him who was nailed to the tree."

He cried out in agony of heart, "Oh, God, I look, I look to Jesus." Then he was carried to the top of the waves and lost consciousness.

Hours afterwards when the storm had ceased and the men came out to clear the deck, they found him lying unconscious, crowded up against a bulwark. Evidently, while one wave had carried him off the deck, another had carried him back again. The sailors took him into the cabin and gave him restoratives. When he came to, the first words from his lips were, "Thank God, I'm saved!"

From that time on he had an assurance of God's salvation that meant everything to him.

Then his mother told him how she had prayed for him that night. They realized that it was just at the time when he was in such desperate circumstances, and God had heard and answered.

Now suppose that that young man's body had never been brought back to the ship. Suppose he had sunk down into the depths. People might have thought he was lost forever in his sin, but he would have been as truly saved as he actually was. God had permitted him to come back in testimony of His wonderful grace.

20

The Preacher and
Fried Chicken

"Look not every man on his own
things, but every man also on the
things of others" (Phil. 2:4).

I have never been able to forget a story I heard evangelist Paul Rader relate on one occasion. I may not now be able to recall all the details, but so nearly as I remember, it was as follows:

Mr. Rader mentioned having known three ministers, all of whom came from a particular part of the South and were all characterized by a spirit of intense self-abnegation and kindly interest in the needs of others. To one of these Mr. Rader said, "I have known two other men from your part of the country and you have all commended yourselves to me by your unselfishness. How come that you are all so much alike?"

Modestly the preacher answered, "If we have any such marks as you speak of, we owe our unselfishness to a circuit-rider. When we were just boys he used to come to our section every two weeks."

He then went on to describe him as a lean, cadaverous-looking man of the Abraham Lincoln type who, on the first Sunday he preached in the country schoolhouse, gave a sermon in the morning and another in the afternoon. Between the services the ladies of the congregation served a picnic lunch in the open air. Great platters of fried chicken, ham, and other meats were laid out on gleaming white tablecloths; these were surrounded by stacks of biscuits, corn pone, hard-boiled eggs, cakes and other delicacies. When all was ready, the assembled group sat down on the greensward to enjoy the repast.

A number of lively boys were always at the front, hoping to get nearest to the platter of chicken. But on this particular occasion, so great was the crowd, the boys were told to wait until their elders were all served. Angrily they went off back of a nearby shed and indulged in the pastime of shooting dice, in revenge for the unkind way they felt they had been treated. They appointed one lad as a watcher, to keep tab on the way the viands were disappearing.

Ruefully, he told of piles of chicken disappearing: still, more came in from nearby wagons. Suddenly, in great excitement he exclaimed, "Say, look at that preacher! The old squirrel! He's eaten all he could and now when he thinks no one sees him, he's filling those big pockets in the tail of his long coat." All looked angrily and saw it was indeed true.

Just then one of the women exclaimed, "Why, look at the preacher's plate. You all are neglecting him. Hand over the fried chicken." And she heaped his plate up with appetizing pieces; he nibbled a few minutes — then surreptitiously took two bandana handkerchiefs out of each breast pocket and, filling them with select pieces, stored them away.

Rising with the rest, the preacher backed off, as the boys thought, to hide his "loot" in his baggage. But after moving away from the crowd he turned, and hurried down to the back of the barn where the angry boys were waiting for the second call to lunch. "Boys," he exclaimed, "I was afraid they were forgetting you, so I saved a lot of the white meat and the drumsticks for you." Out came the four clean handkerchiefs and he passed the tender morsels around. The boys were captured. Amazed, they eagerly accepted the proffered dainties.

"This was characteristic of that preacher," said Mr. Rader's friend. "We felt we had found a real friend—a man who loved other people better than he loved himself. He could do anything with us. He led us all to Christ during the years of his ministry among us, sent several out as foreign missionaries, and we three into the ministry at home. It was the unselfish spirit he manifested that gripped our hearts and won our confidence; so that his sermons reached our consciences and brought us to know his Saviour as ours."

21
The Two Natures

"The flesh lusteth against the Spirit,
and the Spirit against the flesh: and
these are contrary the one to the
other" (Gal. 5:17).

An American Indian was giving his testimony in a gathering of Christian members of his tribe. He told of his conversion and of how in the beginning he felt as though he would never sin again; he was so happy in knowing His Saviour. But, he explained, as time went on he became conscious of an inward conflict, which he described somewhat as follows:

"It seems, my brothers, that I have two dogs fighting in my heart: one is a very good dog, a beautiful white dog, and he is always watching out for my best interests. The other is a very bad dog, a black dog, who is always trying to destroy the things I want to see built up. These dogs give me a lot of trouble because they are always quarreling and fighting with each other."

One of his hearers looked up and asked laconically,

"Which one wins?" The other instantly replied, "Which-ever one I say 'Sic 'im' to."

Surely there could not be a more apt illustration of the two natures in the believer. "If we walk in the Spirit we shall not fulfill the lusts of the flesh." But if we pander to the flesh, we will be certain to go down in defeat.

22
Accepted in the Beloved

"He hath made us accepted in the beloved" (Eph. 1:6).

Years ago I was preaching in the small town of Roosevelt, Washington, on the north bank of the Columbia River. I was the guest of friends who were sheep-raisers. It was lambing time and every morning we went out to see the lambs—hundreds of them—playing about on the green. One morning I was startled to see an old ewe go loping across the road, followed by the strangest looking lamb I had ever beheld. It apparently had six legs, and the last two were hanging helplessly as though paralyzed, and the skin seemed to be partially torn from its body in a way that made me feel the poor little creature must be suffering terribly. But when one of the herders caught the lamb and brought it over to me, the mystery was explained. That lamb did not really belong originally to that ewe. She had a lamb which was bitten by a rattlesnake and died. This lamb that I saw was an orphan and needed a mother's care. But at first the bereft ewe refused to have anything to do with it. She sniffed at it when it was brought to her, then pushed it away, saying as plainly as a sheep could say it, "That is not our family odor!" So the herders skinned the lamb that had died and very carefully drew the fleece over the living lamb. This left the hind-leg coverings dragging loose. Thus covered, the lamb was brought again to the ewe. She smelled it once more and this time seemed thoroughly satisfied and adopted it as her own.

It seemed to me to be a beautiful picture of the grace of God to sinners. We are all outcasts and have no claim upon His love. But God's own Son, the "Lamb of God, that taketh away the sin of the World," has died for us and now we who believe are dressed up in the fleece of the Lamb who died. Thus, God has accepted us in Him, and "there is therefore now no condemnation to them which are in Christ Jesus." We are as dear to the heart of the Father as His own holy, spotless Son.

> "So dear, so very dear to God,
>   More dear I cannot be;
> The love wherewith He loves His Son,
>   Such is His love to me,
> So near, so very near to God,
>   Nearer I could not be,
> For in the person of His Son,
>   I am as near as He."

23
Cobbling for the Glory of God

"Do all in the name of the Lord
Jesus" (Col. 3:17).

When I was a boy, I felt it was both a duty and
a privilege to help my widowed mother make ends meet
by finding employment in vacation time, on Saturdays
and other times when I did not have to be in school. For
quite a while I worked for a Scottish shoemaker, or "cobbler," as he preferred to be called, an Orkney man, named
Dan Mackay. He was a forthright Christian and his little
shop was a real testimony for Christ in the neighborhood.
The walls were literally covered with Bible texts and
pictures, generally taken from old-fashioned Scripture
Sheet Almanacs, so that look where one would, he
found the Word of God staring him in the face. There
were John 3:16 and John 5:24, Romans 10:9, and many
more.

On the little counter in front of the bench on which
the owner of the shop sat, was a Bible, generally open,

and a pile of gospel tracts. No package went out of that shop without a printed message wrapped inside. And whenever opportunity offered, the customers were spoken to kindly and tactfully about the importance of being born again and the blessedness of knowing that the soul is saved through faith in Christ. Many came back to ask for more literature or to inquire more particularly as to how they might find peace with God, with the blessed results that men and women were saved, frequently right in the shoeshop.

It was my chief responsibility to pound leather for shoe soles. A piece of cowhide would be cut to suit, then soaked in water. I had a flat piece of iron over my knees and, with a flat-headed hammer, I pounded these soles until they were hard and dry. It seemed an endless operation to me, and I wearied of it many times.

What made my task worse was the fact that, a block away, there was another shop that I passed going and coming to or from my home, and in it sat a jolly, godless cobbler who gathered the boys of the neighborhood about him and regaled them with lewd tales that made him dreaded by respectable parents as a menace to the community. Yet, somehow, he seemed to thrive and that perhaps to a greater extent than my employer, Mackay. As I looked in his window, I often noticed that he never pounded the soles at all, but took them from the water, nailed them on, damp as they were, and with the water splashing from them as he drove each nail in.

One day I ventured inside, something I had been warned never to do. Timidly, I said, "I notice you put the soles on while still wet. Are they just as good as if they were pounded?" He gave me a wicked leer as he answered, "They come back all the quicker this way, my boy!"

Feeling I had learned something, I related the instance to my boss and suggested that I was perhaps wasting time in drying out the leather so carefully. Mr. Mackay stopped his work and opened his Bible to the passage that reads, "Whatsoever ye do, do all to the glory of God."

"Harry," he said, "I do not cobble shoes just for the four bits or six bits (50¢ or 75¢) that I get from my customers. I am doing this for the glory of God. I expect to see every shoe I have ever repaired in a big pile at the judgment seat of Christ, and I do not want the Lord to say to me in that day, 'Dan, this was a poor job. You did not do your best here.' I want Him to be able to say, 'Well done, good and faithful servant.'"

Then he went on to explain that just as some men are called to preach, so he was called to fix shoes, and that only as he did this well would his testimony count for God. It was a lesson I have never been able to forget. Often when I have been tempted to carelessness, and to slipshod effort, I have thought of dear, devoted Dan Mackay, and it has stirred me up to seek to do all as for Him who died to redeem me.

24
Law and Grace

"We are not under the law, but under
grace" (Rom. 6:15).

Some years ago, I had a little school for young
Indian men and women, who came to my home in Oakland, California, from the various tribes in northern Arizona. One of these was a Navajo young man of unusually keen intelligence. One Sunday evening, he went with me to our young people's meeting. They were talking about the Epistle to the Galatians, and the special subject was law and grace. They were not very clear about it, and finally one turned to the Indian and said, "I wonder whether our Indian friend has anything to say about this."

He rose to his feet and said, "Well, my friends, I have been listening very carefully, because I am here to learn all I can in order to take it back to my people. I do not understand all that you are talking about, and I do not think you do yourselves. But concerning this law and grace business, let me see if I can make it clear. I think it is like this. When Mr. Ironside brought me from my

237

home we took the longest railroad journey I ever took. We got out at Barstow, and there I saw the most beautiful railroad station and hotel I have ever seen. I walked all around and saw at one end a sign, 'Do not spit here.' I looked at that sign and then looked down at the ground and saw many had spitted there, and before I think what I am doing I have spitted myself. Isn't that strange when the sign says, 'Do not spit here'?

"I come to Oakland and go to the home of the lady who invited me to dinner today and I am in the nicest home I have ever been in. Such beautiful furniture and carpets, I hate to step on them. I sank into a comfortable chair, and the lady said, 'Now, John, you sit there while I go out and see whether the maid has dinner ready.' I look around at the beautiful pictures, at the grand piano, and I walk all around those rooms. I am looking for a sign; the sign I am looking for is, 'Do not spit here,' but I look around those two beautiful drawing rooms, and cannot find a sign like this. I think, 'What a pity when this is such a beautiful home to have people spitting all over it — too bad they don't put up a sign!' So I look all over that carpet, but cannot find that anybody has spitted there. What a queer thing! Where the sign says, 'Do not spit,' a lot of people spitted. Where there was no sign at all, in that beautiful home, nobody spitted. Now I understand! That sign is law, but inside the home it is grace. They love their beautiful home, and they want to keep it clean. They do not need a sign to tell them so. I think that explains the law and grace business."

As he sat down, a murmur of approval went round the room and the leader exclaimed, "I think that is the best illustration of law and grace I have ever heard."

25
The New Man

"Whosoever is born of God doth not
commit [that is, practice] sin; for his
seed remaineth in him: and he cannot
sin, because he is born of God"
(I John 3:9).

It is the grace of God working in the soul that
makes the believer delight in holiness, in righteousness,
in obedience to the will of God, for real joy is found in
the service of the Lord Jesus Christ. I remember a man
who lived a life of gross sin.

After his conversion, one of his old friends said to
him, "Bill, I pity you—a man that has been such a high-
flier as you. And now you have settled down; you go to
church, or stay at home and read the Bible and pray; you
never have good times any more."

"But, Bob," said the man, "you don't understand. I
get drunk every time I want to. I go to the theater every
time I want to. I go to the dance when I want to. I play
cards and gamble whenever I want to."

"I say, Bill," said his friend, "I didn't understand it

that way. I thought you had to give up these things to be a Christian."

"No, Bob," said Bill, "the Lord took the 'want to' out when He saved my soul, and He made me a new creature in Christ Jesus."

When we are born of God we receive a new life and that life has its own new nature, a nature that hates sin and impurity and delights in holiness and goodness.

26

In the Cleft of the Rock

"Call upon me in the day of trouble: I
will deliver thee" (Ps. 50:15).

Years ago, while working among the Laguna Indians, we were asked to speak at a little village called
Pawate. It was in the days before automobiles, and we
rode in large wagons drawn by horses for some fourteen
miles over rough roads until we reached the village. We
had a meeting in the afternoon, and Indians from all
about gathered. We started back at 4:30 or 5 o'clock
because we were to have a meeting at Casa Blanca that
night. We had not gone very far when we saw a terrible
storm was about to break over us. Soon we could see the
rain was pouring down at a distance and driving rapidly
toward us.

I said, "We are certainly going to get soaked."

Our driver replied, "I hope not. I think we can make
the rock before the storm reaches us. There is a great
rock ahead; and if we can make it, we will be sheltered."

We hurried on and soon saw a vast rock rising right up from the plain, perhaps forty or fifty feet in height, covering possibly an acre or more of ground. As we drew near, we saw a great cave in the rock. Instead of stopping to unhitch the horses, our driver drove right into the cave, and, in another minute or two, the storm broke over the rock in all its fury.

While the storm raged outside, one of the Indians struck up, in the Laguna tongue, "Rock of Ages, cleft for me, let me hide myself in Thee," and we realized the meaning of the poet's words then as perhaps never before.

27

A Butterfly Used
to Answer Prayer

"Is there any thing too hard for me?"
(Jer. 32:27).

An English evangelist, whom I have learned to know and love, Mr. H. P. Barker, tells an interesting story of a poor woman who was being pressed by a tradesman to pay an account which she knew she had already settled. In that case he demanded that she produce a receipt; quite certain she had received one she hunted and hunted, but was absolutely unable to find it. She went through piles of papers and letters, but to no avail—the receipt was not forthcoming. Finally the tradesman came to her again and made a very angry demand upon her for immediate payment.

In her distress she turned to the Lord in earnest prayer, asking Him to bring the receipt to light. Then in a moment or two, a butterfly flew into the room through an open window, and her little boy, eager to catch the beautiful creature, ran after it. The frightened insect flew over to the wall on one side and down behind a trunk. The boy in his eagerness to catch it, pushed out the trunk, and there, behind it on the floor lay the missing receipt! Snatching it up triumphantly, the poor widow showed it to the tradesman, who went away discomfited. As his own handwriting declared, the debt had been paid.

Who can doubt but that He who notes the sparrow's fall and who would have us learn lessons from the ant and the coney and other small creatures, directed even the movements of a butterfly in order that He might answer His handmaiden's prayer!

28

"I'm In for a Good Time"

"She that liveth in pleasure is dead
while she liveth" (I Tim. 5:6).

Some years ago, I had been preaching Christ as
God's remedy for man's ruined condition, to the hardy
population of a beautiful mining town in the mountain
regions of Northern California. One afternoon I noticed
in the meeting-hall a young woman whose sin-marked
face, weary look and careless demeanor could not fail to
attract attention.

Stepping over to her at the close, I asked, "What
about your soul? Have you ever thought of preparing for
eternity?"

"My soul?—I ain't got none," was the flippant reply,
accompanied by a foolish laugh. Further conversation
seemed to make no impression, for, after solemnly warning her of coming judgment, she exclaimed, "You ain't
going to scare me into religion. Wouldn't I look nice
joining you folks? I'm in for a good time."

"But when you've had your day, when your so-called good time is over forever, when death, judgment, and eternity have to be faced, when God has to be met, *what then?*"

"Oh, well, of course, I don't intend to live like this right along, I'll get religion when I grow old. I ain't got time for it now."

"Yes; so the devil has deceived thousands, but you may never live to grow old. You may not have time to prepare for eternity, though you must find time to die."

Another laugh greeted this warning, and she was gone. It seemed almost impossible that so young a person could be so hardened. I was told she had abandoned herself to a grossly wicked life, though little more than a child, and was an outcast from respectable society. Alas, how sin degrades, hardens, and blinds its poor victims!

Some weeks after the above conversation, an undertaker came to the house where I was staying; he said that he had a funeral to conduct that was a source of much embarrassment to him. The person to be buried was a young woman of so notorious a character that he could scarcely persuade anyone to act as pall-bearers. Mentioning her name, he asked if we knew any who might do her this last service. We promptly offered ourselves. That would do. Some former companions of her folly had already promised to be the others.

It was the girl I had so recently spoken to, cut down in a moment — "suddenly destroyed, and that without remedy." Two days earlier, after a public holiday spent in a revolting manner, she was borne home drunk and put into a bed, from which she never arose. In a few hours she had passed into eternity, having died in great agony from the baneful effects of her long debauch. The wine-cup and its accompaniments had claimed another victim.

Awful was the sight of her pale, swollen face. A minister had been called in, but what could he say? What comfort could he give? Of death-bed repentance even he could not speak. No hope could he hold out that she might after all be saved. She had been asked by her mother if she wanted someone to come in to pray with her. "No," she said, "no one." "Couldn't she remember a prayer, then, to say herself—the Lord's prayer, or any other?" "No, I can't"; and instead of prayer there were oaths and groans of anguish. "She had lived her life," the minister said, "I shall not speak of it, for it cannot be altered now. You have *yours* to live yet. I speak then to *you,*" and he faithfully urged them to flee to Christ alone for refuge.

As I helped to lower the coffin into the grave, my heart was sad indeed. As I turned away, I heard some one exclaim, under his breath, "Just think of it, only seventeen years old, and gone to—!" The last word was lost in the noise about me, or perhaps never uttered.

Excerpts from
The Midnight Cry

The Midnight Cry
  *The Evidence that the Church of God
  Is About to Close its Earthly History*

  *The Evidence that the Times of the
  Gentiles Have Nearly Run Their Course*

29

The Midnight Cry

PART I: The Evidence that the Church of God Is About to Close Its Earthly History

Even in apostolic days the near return of the Lord Jesus was ever kept before the souls of believers as a present hope; yet there are many scriptures that in a hidden way (as we can *now* realize) intimated a certain series of events, or succession of conditions, which would run their course ere the blessed hope was fulfilled. In the wisdom of God these prophetic forecasts of the Church's history were couched in terms of such a nature as not to hinder Christians of any period in their continued expectancy of the Lord's coming, which was designed to be a great sheet-anchor to their souls, keeping them from drifting into worldliness and kindred folly.

But now that nearly twenty centuries (two of God's great "days"—II Peter 3:8) have elapsed, we can look back over the long course of the Church's pilgrimage and see how all her varied states and experiences were foreknown and foretold, and the heart thrills with joyful expectancy as we look ahead. For the next great miraculous event *must* be the shining forth of the Morning

251

Star, "the coming of the Lord Jesus, and our gathering together unto Him."

I purpose to trace this out from several different standpoints. In our introduction we have noticed briefly how the Lord Himself intimated what has been mentioned in the parable of the ten virgins. It was a veiled picture of the whole course of Christendom, and plainly divides the Church dispensation into three distinct stages, or epochs: First, the period of eager expectation. Second, the era of lethargic indifference to the blessed hope. Third, the season of awakening which was the almost immediate precursor of the coming of the Bridegroom. We are living in this last solemn time, and it is well to be trimming our lamps and waiting in holy fear from the summons which may come at any moment to enter in with Him to the Marriage Supper of the Lamb.

The parable of the Ten Virgins was not given, it is true, to teach Church truth, but it presents in a graphic way the responsibility of saints to wait for the return of the Lord.

There are other passages corroborative of this interpretation, and to them let us now turn.

In the two Epistles to Timothy we have two distinct conditions predicted as characterizing what the Holy Spirit designates "the latter times" and "the last days." In I Timothy 4:1– 5 He speaks of the first of these periods; in II Timothy 3:1– 9, of the second. A careful reading of both passages ought, I think, to convince any reader that they show the progress of evil.

At any rate, the conditions of the "latter times" were the first to develop, and out of these grew the anarchic state of the "last days."

I quote the first scripture in full: "Now the Spirit speaketh expressly, that in the latter times some shall depart from the faith, giving heed to seducing spirits, and doctrines of demons; speaking lies in hypocrisy; having their conscience seared [*Gk.,* cauterized]; forbidding to marry, and commanding to abstain from foods, which God hath created to be received with thanksgiving of those who believe and know the truth. For every creature of God is good, and nothing to be refused, if it be received with thanksgiving; for it is sanctified by the word of God and prayer" (KJV, 1911).

Now while the various things here credited to demoniacal influence are found in many modern systems, such as Christian Science, Seventh-day Adventism, and others, it is very evident that it was in connection with the Romish apostasy they were first introduced. The "latter times" were the times of Papal domination. Their evil teachings are still to be found on many sides, but the point I want to make is that the latter times have long since been passed, and we are further down the course of time than many have supposed.

Note well how Rome has fulfilled these predictions to the letter. Departing from the faith of God's word, she has been misled by evil spirits seducing her devotees to believe that the church cannot err, and that her voice is the voice of inspiration. Thus has Satan foisted doctrines of demons on the blinded nations. Rome, the very citadel of untruth, has spoken lies in hypocrisy, her leaders having cauterized consciences which seemed immune to all Scriptural appeals. This the Reformation proved, when God "gave her space to repent . . . and she repented not" (Rev. 2:21).

But one might say: "All this is mere assumption. You tell us Rome is demon-led. You tell us her hierarchy teach lies in hypocrisy. But this is the very point to be proven. What outward evidence have you that she is the guilty one?"

In reply we turn to I Timothy 4:3, where God has

given us two great marks which none can successfully deny fit Rome, as they fully describe no other large communion. It was Rome who forbade to marry—enjoining the unnatural celibacy upon her vast clergy and her hosts of monks and nuns, thus setting herself up to be wiser than God (who says: "Marriage is honorable in all," Heb. 13:4), belittling His holy ordinance of matrimony, declaring the celibate nun far holier than the married mother, and the unwedded priest in a higher state of grace than the godly husband and father.

And what of the second mark? Who has so assiduously cultivated the dogma that piety is manifested in abstention from certain foods, as Rome? God created all to be received with thanksgiving. Rome would damn the one who ate flesh on Fridays and gave God thanks therefor! Her numberless rules on such subjects declare all too plainly that she it is who is marked out in I Timothy 4:1–5. Others have been deluded by the same demons, but it was in the Roman apostasy that the "latter times" came in.

Now let us turn to the second Epistle: "This know also, that in the last days perilous times shall come. For men shall be self-lovers, moneylovers, boasters, proud, blasphemers, disobedient to parents, unthankful, unholy, without natural affection, unforgiving, false accusers, incontinent, savage, haters of good, traitors, heady, highminded, lovers of pleasures rather than lovers of God; having a form of godliness, but denying the power thereof; from such turn away. For of this sort are they who creep into houses, and lead captive silly women laden with sins, led away with manifold desires, ever learning and never able to come to the knowledge of the truth. Now as Jannes and Jambres withstood Moses, so do these also resist the truth: men of corrupt minds, reprobate concerning the faith. But they shall proceed no further:

for their folly shall be manifest unto all, as theirs also was" (KJV, 1911).

These are the great outstanding features of the "last days"—closing the Church dispensation, and to be immediately followed by the coming of the Lord. Can any believer in Holy Writ doubt our being now in the very midst of them?

But it may be here objected: "When have men in general been other than as here depicted? Is not this but a repetition of what Paul has already said in describing the heathen world in his day? (Rom. 1:29–32). In what special sense are they any more characteristic now than then?" To these very natural queries I reply: "Such things, indeed, ever described the heathen; but in II Timothy 3 the Holy Spirit is describing conditions in *the professing Church* in the last days! It is not the openly wicked and godless who are being depicted here. It is those who have a form of godliness, while denying its power. *This* is what makes the passage so intensely solemn and gives it such tremendous weight in the present day. There are twenty-one outstanding features in this depicting of Church conditions in the last days, and that each may have its due weight with my reader I touch briefly on them in order.

1. "Men shall be lovers of their ownselves." It is men self-occupied, as contrasted with the godly of all ages who found their joy and delight in looking away from self to God as seen in Christ. This is the age of the egotist in matters spiritual as well as carnal. They find their God "within" them, we are told, and not without. They make no secret of it. When they profess to love God it is *themselves* they love.

2. "Covetous." Is it necessary to speak of this? Colossal fortunes heaped together by men who profess to believe the Bible and its testimony! What a spectacle

for angels and demons! There was one Simon Magus of old. He has myriads of successors in the professing church to-day, and the command "not to eat" with a covetous man or an extortioner is in most places a dead letter indeed.

3. "Boasters." Read the so-called Christian papers; attend Christendom's great coventions of young people, or old. Listen to the great pulpiteers of the day. What is their theme? "Rich and increased with goods and have need of nothing!" Great swelling words are rapturously applauded by people dwelling in a fool's paradise, even when uttered by men who are tearing the Bible to shreds, and who deny practically every truth that it contains.

4. "Proud." So proud as to glory in their shame— congratulating themselves on the very things the Word of God so unsparingly condemns. Proud of their fancied superiority; proud of their eloquence; proud of their miscalled culture; proud of their very impiety, which is hailed as the evidence of broad-mindedness and a cultivated intellect! How nauseating it must all be to Him who said, "Take my yoke upon you and learn of me, for I am meek and lowly in heart."

5. "Blasphemers." Yes, there it is—that big, ugly word that one hesitates to use, but which is chosen by the Holy Spirit Himself to describe the men drawing salaries as ministers of Christ who use their office to impiously deny His name! Blasphemers! Aye, the whole host of the new theologians, miscalled "higher critics," and all their ilk—all who deny the deity of the Son, His virgin-birth, His holy humanity—blasphemers, every one, and as such to be judged unsparingly in the harvest of wrath so near at hand! And think of the disloyalty to Christ of Christians—real Christians, I mean—who can sit and listen to such men week after week, and are too timid to pro-

test, or too indifferent to obey the word, "From such turn away!"

6. "Disobedient to parents." It is one of the crowning sins of the age, and indicates the soon breaking-up of the whole social fabric as at present constituted. Opposition to authority is undoubtedly one of the characteristic features of the times. Children will not brook restraint, and parents have largely lost the sense of their responsibility toward the rising generation. Does this seem unduly pessimistic? Nevertheless, a little thoughtful consideration will, I am sure, convince any reasonable person of its truth. And it may be laid down as an axiom, that children not trained in obedience to parents will not readily be obedient to God. We have been sowing the wind in this respect for years, as nations and as families. The reaping of the whirlwind is certain to follow.

7. "Unthankful." It is the denial of divine Providence—utterly forgetting the Source of all blessings, both temporal and spiritual. Straws indicate the turn of the wind, and even in "so small a matter," as some may call it, as the giving-up of the good old-fashioned and eminently scriptural custom of thanksgiving at the table, we may see how prevalent is the sin of unthankfulness among professed Christians. Go into the restaurants or other eating-houses; how often can you tell the believer from the unbeliever?

8. "Unholy." The godly separation from the world according to the Bible is sneered at as "bigotry" and "Puritanism." In its place has come a jolly, rollicking worldliness that ill comports with the Christian profession. Piety—that characteristic Christian virtue—how little seen now! It is not necessary to be outwardly vile to be unholy. Giving up the line of separation between the believer and the unbeliever is unholiness.

9. "Without natural affection." The foundations of

family life are being destroyed. Unscriptural divorces and all their kindred evils cast their dark shadows over the professing church, as well as over the body politic.

Of the next unholy octave I need not write particularly. To enumerate them is enough to stir the heart and appall the soul when it is remembered how they are tolerated and spreading through the great professing body. 10—"trucebreakers"; 11—"false accusers" (Let us beware lest we be found almost unwittingly in this Satanic company!); 12—"incontinent"; 13—"fierce"; 14—"despisers of those that are good"; 15—"traitors"; 16—"heady"; 17—"highminded." This last accounts largely for the daring things proudly uttered by learned doctors against the Scriptures and the great fundamentals of the faith, and complacently accepted by unregenerate hearers. Surely, the time *has* come "when they will not bear sound teaching, but according to their own desire shall heap to themselves teachers, having itching ears" (II Tim. 4:3, KJV, 1911).

18. "Lovers of pleasures more than lovers of God." Would you not almost think the words were written by some fiery-souled exhorter of the present day? How aptly they characterize in one brief clause the greatest outstanding feature of the religious word. The Church of God has gone into the entertainment business! People must be amused, and as the Church needs the people's money, the Church must, perforce, supply the demand and meet the craving! How else are godless hypocrites to be held together? How otherwise can the throngs of unconverted youths and maidens be attracted to the "services"? So the picture-show and the entertainment, in the form of *musicale* (sacred, perhaps!) and minstrel-show, take the place of the gospel address and the solemn worship of God. And thus Christless souls are lulled to sleep and made to feel "religious" while gratifying

every carnal desire under the sanction of the sham called the Church! — And the end? What an awakening!

19. "Having a form of godliness, but denying the power thereof." Men must have some form of religious expression, and so the outward thing is sustained after the life is gone out of it. Thus formality prevails where regeneration, conversion to God, the spirit's sanctification, and everything really vital has long since been virtually denied. The bulk of so-called church-members do not even profess to have been saved, or to be Spirit-indwelt. All this is foreign to their mode of thought or speech. The gospel, which alone is "the power of God unto salvation," is seldom preached, and, by the mass, never missed! Could declension and apostasy go much further? Yet there are still lower depths to be sounded!

20. Feminism. No, you won't find the word — but read verse 6 again, slowly and thoughtfully. Does it not indicate a great feminist movement in these last dark days? "Silly women, laden with sins, led away with divers lusts" — craving what God in His infinite wisdom has forbidden them: authority, publicity, masculinity, and what not? Thus they leave their own estate and make a new religion to suit themselves. Is it a matter of no import that just such emotional, insubject women were the tools used by Satan for the starting and propagating of so many modern fads? Need one mention Mesdames Blavatsky, Besant and Tingley of Theosophy; the Fox sisters' relation to modern Spiritism; Mrs. Mary Baker Glover Eddy and her host of female practitioners in the woman's religion miscalled "Christian Science"; the neurotic Ellen G. White and her visionary system of "Seventh-day Adventism"; Ella Wheeler Wilcox and her associates in the spreading of what they have been pleased to denominate the "New Thought," which is only the devil's old lie, "Ye shall be as gods," in a modern garb;

and, the women-expounders of the "Silent Unity," or "Home of Truth" delusions? All these are outside the "orthodox" fold; but when we look within, what a large place has the modern feminist movement secured in the affections of women who profess to believe the Bible, but who unblushingly denounce Paul as "an old bachelor" with narrow, contracted ideas, little realizing that they are thereby rejecting the testimony of the Holy Spirit. It is one of the signs of the times, and clearly shows towards what the professing body is so rapidly drifting!

21. "Ever learning, and never able to come to the knowledge of the truth"—and that by *their own* confession. They are "truth-seekers." Ask them if it be not so. They confess it without a blush, and consider it humility thus to speak. According to these apostates, the Church which began as the "pillar and ground of the truth," is, in this twentieth century of its existence, "seeking" the truth, thereby acknowledging they never yet have found it! Truth-seekers! Yet the Lord Jesus said, "I am the Way, the TRUTH, and the Life." Why then seek further? Because they have drifted away from Him and His Word, so they go on, ever learning, ever seeking, and ever missing the glorious revelation of the TRUTH as it is in Jesus.

Predictions of two directly opposite conditions are made in the Word of God in regard to events to be consummated immediately before the Lord's return to establish his kingdom and close up the Times of the Gentiles. If therefore we see these predictions within a small degree of being already fulfilled prior to the rapture of the Church, we may be certain that the coming of the Saviour to the air is very near at hand.

The predictions referred to were made—one directly by the Lord Himself; the other by the Holy Spirit through the apostle Paul. To the question of the disciples, "What shall be the sign of Thy coming and of the end of the age?" the Lord gave a lengthy answer recorded in Matthew, chapters 24 and 25; but the prediction I refer to now is that of the fourteenth verse of chapter 24: "This gospel of the kingdom shall be preached in all the world for a witness unto all the nations; *and then shall the end come.*" Now I recognize, in common with others, a distinction in *aspect* between "the gospel of the kingdom" and "the gospel of the grace of God," but I regard it as a mistake to say that the gospel of the kingdom is not, or should not be, preached *now*. Each are but different aspects of the one gospel; and Paul preached both.

In Acts 20:24, 25 we find the two aspects intimately connected in the ministry of the apostle Paul: "none of these things move me, neither count I my life dear unto myself, so that I might finish my course with joy, and the ministry which I have received of the Lord Jesus, to testify *the gospel of the grace of God.* And now, behold, I know that ye all, among whom I have gone *preaching the kingdom of God,* shall see my face no more." See also Acts 14:22. When he wrote, "If thou shalt confess with thy mouth the Lord Jesus," it involved the present phase of the gospel of the kingdom; when he added, "And believe in thy heart that God hath raised Him from the dead, thou shalt be saved," it was the gospel of the grace of God. Christ Jesus is *Lord.* He is also *Redeemer.* Men are called on to own Him in both characters. In the Jewish age, and in the coming tribulation period, the gospel of the *kingdom* is the emphatic phase. Now, where there is intelligence, it is the *grace* of God that the gospel preacher will lay special stress upon.

Now it is the individual believer who owns the sovereignty of the Lord Jesus Christ. In the Tribulation era, when Matthew 24:14 will be completely carried out, the whole world will be called on to own the sway of Him who is about to appear as King of kings and Lord of lords to reign over His world-kingdom.

But why this effort to show that the gospel of the kingdom is *now* being preached? Because, my reader, the *end* comes when it has been carried into all the world, for a witness! And even now it has gone to the uttermost parts of the earth, so that it can confidently be said that with the possible exception of a few *wild* tribes of Indians in South America, or negroes in Africa, there is probably no nation to whom the witness has not already been given. The nineteenth was the greatest missionary century since the days of the apostles. In one hundred years, the gospel was practically carried to the whole world after a millennium of lethargy and indifference to the claims of the heathen. This great missionary awakening is like the trumpet-blasts that herald the King's approach. In this twentieth century the work of carrying the gospel to the pagan world has gone on more extensively than ever. None can say when the last tribe or nation will get the witness message, but when they do, *"then* shall the end come." And, mark it well, it is not before the rapture, but after it, that the final call is to be given. It will be Jewish saints, and not Christian missionaries, who will complete the work of world-wide evangelization; therefore the coming of the Lord as predicted in I Thessalonians 4 must be very near!

But now we turn to consider the other prediction to which I referred in the beginning. "That day," writes the apostle, "shall not come except there come the apostasy first" (literal rendering of II Thess. 2:3). This is startling surely—the gospel going into all the world, the apostasy sweeping all before it, and both just before the end, or the day of the Lord, shall come! How strange a paradox, and yet how exactly are both scriptures being fulfilled!

Never before such wide-spread missionary activity! Never before such far-reaching apostasy! Earnest workers guided by the Holy Spirit are hazarding their lives to carry the good news of Christ's incarnation, atonement, resurrection and coming again to the heathen world. Equally earnest, but Satan-inspired, men at home are tearing the Bible in pieces and railing at these very truths once for all delivered to the saints, and, alas! their unholy rationalizing is fast finding its way into the fields of missionary endeavor, where education is taking the place of the gospel; and culture, character-building, and various accomplishments are put in place of the Son of God, the Saviour of sinners!

Theological seminaries, in many instances, are hotbeds of infidelity. Schools and colleges are busy, as Harold Bolce graphically expressed it, in "blasting at the Rock of Ages." The rising generation in so-called Christian lands bids fair to be a generation of Bible-rejectors. "The prophets prophesy falsely, and the priests bear rule by their means, and My people love to have it so, and what will ye do in the end thereof?" That *end* is almost upon us, and "When the Son of Man cometh shall He find the faith on the earth?" It is fast being supplanted by human speculations and "oppositions of science falsely so-called."

The leaven of man-worship is rapidly leavening the whole lump and preparing the way for the Antichrist who shall, if it were possible, deceive the very elect. Thank God, it is *not* possible; but it behooves every regenerated soul to hold fast to the revealed Word of God and utterly refuse the lying systems of the enemy. To sit in churches and listen to preachers of the apostasy, or to support such in any way, is treason against Christ! "He that biddeth him [the false teacher] God speed is partaker of his evil deeds."

It would be a great mercy if every converted person would refuse positively to listen twice to a minister who denies the inspiration of the Bible, or to give a penny to a church or a missionary society that gave the right hand of fellowship to men of this type. To stay the on-rushing apostasy is impossible. To protest against it and to "have no fellowship with the unfruitful works of darkness" is a positive duty.

Reader, let me press my point again. The world-wide gospel proclamation and world-wide apostasy *at the same time* are clear proofs that the end is close upon us! It is too late to trifle. Let us be in earnest for the few remaining hours!

Another line of evidence is presented in the seven prophetic letters of Revelation 2 and 3. For that they *are* prophetic, and not merely moral — dispensational, and not simply local in their application — is a fact now familiar to many earnest students of the Scriptures. The proof of this is found in their exact correspondence with the seven stages of the history of the Church on earth. This is incontrovertible, however self-styled optimists may object to it — the objection being chiefly based on the fact that Laodicea closes the septenary series, thus precluding all thought of a triumphant Church and a converted world at the end of the dispensation. Yet the Church shall be triumphant; of that there should be no question. For our Lord Jesus has solemnly declared, "Upon this Rock (Christ as Son of the living God) I will build my Church; and the gates of hell shall not prevail against it." But between the Church of Christ's building and the vast complex church of man's devising there is a great difference. The real Church will be triumphantly raptured to glory ere the judgments fall on the great apostate mass of Laodicea.

I do not therefore attempt to prove by argument that

the seven letters give us an outline of the Church's course
from apostolic days to the closing up of the present age.
This has been so well done by others that it would be
on my part a work of supererogation to try to make it
any more convincing.* I only desire in these necessarily
brief pages to refresh the memory of my reader by point-
ing out how aptly those letters fit the history.

Ephesus then, from this viewpoint, presents the
Church in apostolic days — an unworldly, called-out company who labored earnestly and well in making known
the riches of grace, and who walked apart from iniquity;
unable to bear those who were evil, as indeed these in
turn could not endure the company of God's redeemed,
for we read elsewhere, "Of the rest durst no man join
himself to them." In those days of primitive simplicity
men were tried by the testimony they brought, and if
they spoke not according to the doctrine of Christ were
rejected as "liars" — a "short and ugly word" that aptly
designates many profane hucksters of the Word of God
to-day.

But the picture has its shadows too, for even during
the very lifetime of the apostolic band declension began:
the Church left her first love, and a somewhat mysterious
form of evil, the "deeds of the Nicolaitanes," came in,
though largely against the desire of the mass, for Ephesus is commended because of hatred to this unholy thing.
Leaving their first love was losing the sense of Christ's
presence: occupation with work, with service, took the
place of heart-occupation with Himself. No sect of the
Nicolaitanes is known, though some have tried to link
the name with the reputed followers of an apostate Nicho-
las, traditionally held to be one of the seven men in

* The inquiring reader is referred to "The Prophetic History of the
Church," by F. W. Grant, 35 cts. Same publishers.

Acts 6, who were set apart to serve tables. He is supposed to have taught his disciples that the indulgence of licentious practices was not inconsistent with the grace of God. This, however, is very uncertain and largely conjectural. They seem to be right who consider "Nicolaitanes" to be an untranslated Greek word, properly rendered "rulers of the people." In that case Diotrephes of III John would be a typical Nicolaitane, who has had many successors. It would be the divine condemnation of the clerical system. Not yet had this system become an accepted doctrine, but the deeds manifested the spirit behind it. Crystallization into an accredited dogma came later (Rev. 2:15).

The second period followed apace, as set forth in the letter to Smyrna. It depicts, as by a few master-strokes, the tragedy of the Pagan persecutions in their efforts to crush Christianity beneath the iron heel of the Roman emperors, from Domitian to Diocletian. Nero's persecution was local rather than general, but the monster who succeeded him set in motion a world-wide effort to destroy the Church of Christ. Historians count ten general persecutions, which are connected with ten main edicts of the emperors. The last under Diocletian went on for ten years, ceasing only with the death of the incapacitated tyrant. "Ye shall have tribulation ten days" seems to hint at this. But a suffering Church is more likely to be rich in faith than a Church fawned upon by the world; though in deepest poverty the Church in the Smyrna age was "rich," and prospered, for as Augustine later said, "The blood of the martyrs is the seed of the Church." Those dark days were days of Christian devotion and heroism unparalleled save in similar times of suffering and danger. And yet the picture is not altogether bright, for the clear gospel of grace was largely obscured by the legal teaching of "those who said they were Jews and

were not." Such are a synagogue of Satan. Judaism was
a divine institution, Christianity is a divine revelation.
But the strange mixture of Judaism with Christianity is
of Satan. It is a corruption and a counterfeit; and "the
corruption of the best thing is the worst of corruptions."

Pergamos followed this, and gives us the period of
the Church's relief from persecution and her subsequent
union with the world. It is the era of Constantine the
Great and his successors, when the Church became the
pet of the emperors (save for a brief period under Julian
the Apostate), and Church and State were linked in an
unholy alliance. Thus the Church sat at ease where Satan
had his throne, clung to this for centuries, until the world
itself wearied of her, and wrenched her from her place
of power. He who is familiar with Church history can
scarcely read the Pergamos letter without the vast pag-
eant of the fourth century passing before the eye of his
mind. The death of Diocletian; the temporary triumph
of Maxentius; the Gallic legions hastening eastward led
by Constantine; the famous vision of the fiery cross; the
"in hoc signo vinces" portent; the Christians coming
forth into the glare of publicity from the dens, caves and
catacombs which had been their hiding places for so
long; the bishops summoned to the general's august presence; his endorsement of the new doctrine and intellectual conversion; the cross-led army driving all before it;
the overthrow of Maxentius; Constantine hailed as Emperor of the world; proclaimed head of the heathen church
and *pontifex maximus* (the title of the head of the
hierarchy); the bishops seated among princes; the Church's
mourning over, her eyes dazzled by the unaccustomed
luxury and splendor, basking in the imperial favor! Then
the Arian controversy; Christ's true diety denied, but
maintained at the council of Nicea where despite tremendous pressure the Church "held fast His Name, re-

fusing to deny His faith." Of Antipas personally we know nothing, but we see in his very name (which means "against all") the trumpet note of Athanasius who, when a later Arian emperor sought to persuade him to endorse the hated Unitarian heresy by crying, "All the world is against you," in holy dignity exclaimed, "Then I am *against all* the world."

The Balaam doctrine too was openly advocated by many in those days, and since—urging the mingling of clean and unclean, the unequal yoke of the Church and world, a spiritual marriage, which "Pergamos" seems to imply; while Nicolaitanism, or clerisy, had now become a full-blown doctrine, and the distinction between clergy and laity was at last complete. The Pergamos letter is a synoptic description of the conditions prevailing from the fourth to the seventh centuries.

And Thyatira followed as the natural result. Things were going downhill with fearful rapidity. Yet the church of the middle ages was rich in works of mercy and abounded in "charity." Her monasteries and hostelries dotted the lands and kept open house for the sick and distressed. But doctrinally she had deteriorated tremendously, and the Papal system was fully organized, becoming a church within the Church, to which all had to bow. It was the woman Jezebel teaching and leading the servants of God astray. As the heathen princess of old foisted her idolatry on Israel, so this false paganistic thing crowded out the Christianity of Christ and superseded it by a system unspeakably evil and inherently corrupt.

At the Reformation of the sixteenth century she was "given space to repent, but she repented not," as the decrees of the Council of Trent bear witness. She spurned the light shining from the newly-recovered Scriptures and continued in her idolatrous course. For "her children" there is naught but death, though grace ever has discerned even in Rome a remnant having not known the depths of Satan, whom a gracious Lord owns as His and commands to cling to what they have till He shall come. It is the first intimation that declension has gone so far that His return is now the only hope.

For Sardis, though it speak of Protestantism and its great State churches, is not a true recovery. They had received a deposit of truth at the Reformation, which became crystallized into creeds and confessions but did not quicken the mass. So of the great Protestant bodies it can be said, "Thou hast a name that thou livest and art dead," for churchmanship has largely been substituted for new birth, and orthodoxy for conversion to God. Yet there are a few with garments undefiled who know the Lord and love His truth, and who are exhorted to *watch* for His coming again!

Philadelphia speaks of the great revival period of the eighteenth and nineteenth centuries, assuming different forms in different places, but in all characterized by *reality,* by brotherly love, by clinging to Christ's Word and honoring His Name who is the Holy and the True. They who take such ground will never be popular with the world or the world's churches, but they will be content to know that God approves, and that the Lord Himself has opened for them a door of service which none on earth or anywhere else can shut. They wait in patience for the Morning Star—the Bridegroom's symbolic title.

Laodicea closes the series. It is the solemn arraignment of latitudinarian Christianity with its pride and folly, marked by impudent self-conceit and utter indifference to Christ. It glories in its breadth and culture, its refinements of thought, and its refusal of ancient formulas. It congratulates itself on its wealth and following, while, in His sight who stands knocking outside, it is "poor and wretched and blind and naked." All the church machinery can go on without His presence, and without any sense of His absence.

And this is the last state of the professing body on earth. When things are in this condition, the Lord Himself will come, and will spew out of His mouth that which is so distasteful and disgusting to Him. "After this," says John, "I looked, and behold, a door was opened in heaven." As he is caught up through that open door he beholds surrounding the throne in glory the true Church seated in triumph, as symbolized in the twenty-four elders.

Laodicea is the closing period of the Church's history, and who can doubt that we have now reached the very time depicted? It behooves us to act as men who wait for their Lord, knowing that His coming cannot be much longer delayed.

We have thus glanced at various scriptures having to do with the evidences in the professing church of the Lord's near return. We must now look at some movements among the nations which point unquestionably to the same thing.

PART II: The Evidence that the Times of the Gentiles Have Nearly Run Their Course

The prophetic Scriptures are as a light shining in a dark place. So marvelously has God therein depicted the characteristics of the age in which we live, and the conditions that would prevail as its end drew near, that no reverent reader of the Bible need be left in the dark as to the place now reached in the history of the Gentile powers. Recent startling events are so fully in accord with what Spirit-taught servants of Christ have long seen foretold in Holy Writ as to be overwhelmingly convincing that "all Scripture is given by inspiration of God." He alone sees the end from the beginning and speaks of the things that are not as though they were. It is this feature of foretelling the future that differentiates the Bible from every other book. Human writers guess and theorize. God has by inspiration communicated facts which are attested by each passing year.

In this last respect, the Book of Daniel stands preeminent. The second and third chapters give an outline of the times of the Gentiles from Nebuchadnezzar's day to the setting up of Messiah's kingdom. The four empires of Babylon, Medo-Persia, Greece, and Rome, as depicted in its earlier form, have risen and passed away as foretold. But a later form of the last empire is predicted to arise in the time of the end, immediately before the second coming of the Lord Jesus Christ, the all-glorious Son of Man, as the Stone falling from heaven.

Now the last state of the fourth empire is to be brought about as a result of an effort to combine the iron of imperialism with the miry clay (or, more correctly, brittle pottery) of democracy. This union—which can never be unity—of royal authority and socialistic principles characterizes the feet of the image even before the formation of the ten toes. This latter condition does not come in so long as the Church is still upon earth. It is subsequent to the rapture of the saints of the present dispensation. But the iron and clay are *already in evidence,* and statesmen are making desperate efforts to combine the

two, after having learned, to their chagrin, in the last
hundred or more years, that the "voice of the people,"
if not "the voice of God," is yet something to be reckoned
with—is to be acknowledged and appeased if possible.
With our Bibles open to the second chapter of Daniel,
and the records of the present day before us, we do not
hesitate to say that we are now in the iron and clay
period, and at any moment the Lord's assembling shout
may summon all that are Christ's to the skies, after which
the re-formation of the Roman empire in its last Satan-
controlled condition will be a matter of but a very brief
time, for "a short work will the Lord make in the earth."

When, in past years, teachers of the Word of God
have positively declared that the Scriptures foretold a
new socialistic-empire formed of ten great kingdoms, on
the ground of the Roman empire of old, many found it
hard to take such predictions seriously. But the events
of recent years, particularly since 1914, have wrought a
wondrous change in the minds of men as to this. It is
not only that the enlightened Bible believer declares
such *must* be, but the secular press has taken up the
matter, and it is being pointed out that the formation of
a United States of Europe is *absolutely necessary* to
safeguard the interests of all nations and to preserve the
peace of the world. This in itself is a remarkable sign of
the times, and shows how rapidly the end is approaching.

The world war demonstrated the need of some strong
centralized government that could bring order out of the
chaotic conditions which even the League of Nations
seems unable to control. This League is in itself a step—
and a long step—toward that very union of nations predicted by both Daniel and John in Revelation. And the
sudden rise to power of Mussolini is a startling evidence
of how rapidly the kingdom of the Beast may be developed after the Church is gone. Already we hear of the

revival of the Roman Empire, and this modern "man of destiny" declares that Rome shall soon be restored to its ancient splendors and will emulate the Empire of the Caesars in worldly power and glory.

We need, however, to be on our guard against hastily-arrived at and ill-considered conclusions. I have seen in print, and heard it affirmed by many, that Il Duce, Premier Mussolini of Italy, the great Fascist leader, is the predicted Antichrist, the Man of Sin, who should arise at the end of this age. This is quite unwarranted for a number of reasons. Mussolini is a civil leader, not the head of a religious system. Since the last edition of this booklet was published he has brought about a *rapprochement* with the papacy through the Lateran treaty by which the pope is once more recognized as a temporal prince and Roman Catholicism is now the State Church of Italy. This may result in the fulfilment of the seventeenth of Revelation, placing the mystic woman in the saddle, where for a brief time she will again dominate the Roman earth. But the Antichrist is the lamb-like Beast depicted in the last part of the thirteenth chapter. He is the imitation Lamb of God who is to be energized by Satanic power. This one will utterly deny the Father and the Son. "This," says St. John, "is the deceiver and the antichrist." He will be accepted by apostate Christendom and apostate Judaism as the promised Messiah. His seat will be in Palestine; while, in the West, in the revived Roman Empire of the last days, there will be a great civil leader, a Napoleonic "Man of Destiny," who will for a brief time attempt to exercise autocratic sway over the civilized world. Both this leader, called emphatically, "the Beast," and the Antichrist are to act together as the enemies of God and His truth. But they are distinct personalities.

That we are on the eve of great world changes both

statesmen and religious leaders are agreed. The nature of those changes affords endless cause for speculation. For the devout Christian the next stupendous event that shines through the darkness is the coming of our Lord Jesus Christ and our gathering together unto Him. We do not wait for the Antichrist. We look for the Lord from heaven. We are only interested in the signs of the times as they harmonize with the warnings given whereby we may know that the end of the age is approaching.

In the last chapter of the Book of Daniel there are three statements made which also have a bearing on the times in which our lot is cast. The angel says to the prophet: "But thou, O Daniel, shut up the words, and seal the book, even to the time of the end: many shall run to and fro, and knowledge shall be increased" (v. 4). Observe that three things are mentioned here, which if any one of them came to pass without the other two, would be of no real value in determining the question that is before us. But if *all* come to pass at *the same time* we must be convinced that God has spoken, and has pointed out unerringly three signs that the end times are almost upon us.

Note the three predictions: First, The end-times will be characterized by prophetic enlightenment, marvelously unsealing the Book of Daniel, and the visions therein recorded understood by spiritual men. Second, there will be a period of world wide restlessness: men will run to and fro as never before, owing doubtless to new and convenient methods of locomotion and insatiable desire for travel and adventure. Third, there will be a wide diffusion of knowledge—bringing educational advantages to the door of the poorest if there be but an ambition to learn and acquire. Now what are the facts? The last century has been more and more characterized by the very things mentioned. It is not that these things are occasionally fulfilled, but that they are everywhere apparent in the civilized parts of the world. Here then is a three-fold cord that cannot be quickly broken. Insignificant as any one of these facts might seem if it stood alone, *the combination of the three at one and the same time is the startling fact.* Man's day is nearly at an end. The day of the Lord comes on apace!

Now link on to this evidence a New Testament prophecy that clearly applies to the same times. Turn to I Thessalonians 5:2, 3. "For yourselves know perfectly that the day of the Lord so cometh as a thief in the night. For when they shall say, Peace and safety; then sudden destruction cometh upon them, as travail upon a woman with child; and they shall not escape." Here is a strikingly convincing statement, if received in literality as it is written. The day of the Lord is going to break upon the world at some special time, foreknown by God, when men will be talking loudly of Peace and Safety! These are the very themes talked of on every hand for the last decade, and, despite the fearful European tragedy, are heard more loudly today than ever. Men of affairs are loudly proclaiming a coming era of universal peace to be brought in by arbitration, treaties, and the evolutionary forces of society, while the day of the Lord steals on them unawares in overflowing judgments to cut off the ungodly from the earth, at the very time that universal peace and safety become the slogan of a world devoted to destruction. All man's efforts to make this world a happy and peaceful scene, while still rejecting the Lord Jesus Christ, are futile and vain. "There is no peace, saith my God, to the wicked."

It is not to those who wait for the return of His Son from heaven that the day of the Lord comes as a thief in the night, but to those who ignore His Word and despise His grace. "Ye, brethren, are not in darkness, that that day should overtake you as a thief. . . . Therefore let us not sleep, as do others; but let us watch and be sober" (I Thess. 5:4, 6).

And if we would watch intelligently it is necessary that we be able, through familiarity with the Word of God, to discern aright the signs of the times. In three short verses our Lord Himself has given us a marvelous epitome of the conditions that would prevail immediately before the great tribulation. Weigh carefully Matthew 24:5–7, and ask yourself if anything could more aptly describe the days in which we live. "For many shall come in my name, saying, I am Christ; and shall deceive many. And ye shall hear of wars and rumours of wars; see that ye be not troubled; for all these things must come to pass, but the end is not yet. For nation shall rise against nation, and kingdom against kingdom: and there shall be famines, and pestilences, and earthquakes, in divers places." With this, couple the equally pertinent words of Luke 21:25, 26: "And there shall be signs in the sun, and in the moon, and in the stars; and upon the earth distress of nations, with perplexity; the sea and the waves roaring; Men's hearts failing them for fear, and for looking after those things which are coming on the earth: for the powers of heaven shall be shaken."

The context makes it clear that these are the outward evidences of the near approach of the end times. They do not definitely fix the time when the Lord must come. They simply show that the days of vengeance are coming on apace. And one might fearlessly challenge anyone to give us a better description of our own days than we have in these verses, taking brevity into consideration.

Note the leading features of the two passages:

First: many antichrists. It might be said that there has never been a time since the very days of the apostles that this sign has not been manifested; and this I readily admit. But in a certain sense the whole Christian dispensation is marked by all those things predicted by our Lord, for ever since apostolic days men have lived in what John calls "the last hour." The greater part of earth's time or course has been run; only the last hour remains ere the kingdom be ushered in. But while this is so, we gather that the characteristic features of the age will be accentuated at the close. And so it is at the present solemn moment. We hear of antichrists on every hand, and those who are deceived thereby may well be called legion! In all lands these false Christs are found. In America we have witnessed the "powers and signs and lying wonders" connected with the system miscalled Christian Science, which venerated its woman-founder as the second coming of Christ, and holds its false philosophy to be the promised Comforter, thus blaspheming against the Holy Ghost. Lesser lights have flickered and flamed up, then died down, leaving hosts of disappointed dupes, like Dowie, the pseudo-prophet of Chicago; Sanford, the Elijah of New England; Dr. Teed, the Koresh; and others too numerous to mention; and as they pass away, other deceivers take their places, for men would rather believe any lie than God's truth.

When the Persian antichrist, Abbas Effendi, or Abdul Bahai, toured America and Europe, he was welcomed as the forerunner of universal peace and accorded the liberty of proclaiming his propaganda from "Christian" pulpits. And though, like other pretenders before him, he has passed away, his followers still abound in a land of Bibles, and hope by the dissemination of his principles to bring in a millennial condition while refusing the cross!

Some years ago Mrs. Annie Besant, the aged Theosophical leader, formed the Order of the Star of the East, a Theosophical off-shoot, to wait for a great religious leader—a new incarnation of the Spirit of Christ. The mountain has labored and brought forth—Krishnamurti! Yet vast numbers of otherwise intelligent people accept the drivellings of this colorless youth as the very utterances of inspiration!

Other "coming ones," too numerous to mention, engage the thoughts of men. But it is for Antichrist, not the Christ of God, they wait. The Lord of glory, when He comes again, descends from heaven. The false prophet comes from the earth—born in a natural way.

Second: Scripture predicts a period of terrible unrest and internecine warfare as an evidence that the world is entering "the beginning of sorrows." A few years ago men were flattering themselves that the world would never again be desolated by great wars and wholesale slaughter. It was confidently believed that the social consciousness of the laboring class would make it impossible to hurl great armies against each other. Peace propaganda had so educated the people of all civilized nations that war would soon be outlawed. In the very month that the great 1914-1918 European conflict broke out, the organ of the Peace Society published in Toronto, contained an ably written article declaring that war was now an impossibility, and a great world conflict could never occur again! Clergymen, oblivious of prophetic truth as revealed in Scripture, and carried away by the loose, liberal theological systems of the day, were loudly voicing the same empty boast up to the very day that the devastating carnage began.

And now that comparative peace has succeeded to bloody warfare the same unbelieving views are being taught from many pulpits. Yet ever since the signing of the treaty of Versailles the nations have been feverishly preparing for "the next great war"—building navies, enlisting soldiers, storing ammunition—all for what? Universal peace? Nay, but for the wars and rumors of wars of the closing days of this age, and for the great Armageddon conflict yet to be fought out in the land of Palestine, when all nations shall be drawn into the fray. While every Christian should be grateful to God for the comparative peace now enjoyed, it needs to be remembered it is but a temporary truce, for there can be no lasting peace while Christ is rejected—nor until all Gentile dominions are destroyed and He shall come whose right it is to reign.

In the third and fourth places we read of famines and pestilences, the very natural outcome of war, which have reaped fearful harvests since the great world war, though the science and skill of the world are endeavoring to successfully cope with them. Many high-spirited and noble-minded physicians and nurses laid down their lives in the overpowering conflict in trying to hinder the onrushing pestilence, while the charity of the world was strained in its efforts to check the ravages of famine—and what may it not yet be in the near future? The black and pale horses of famine and pestilence always follow the red horse of battle.

In Luke's account we get the fifth sign that the end is drawing near, calamities such as the world has never previously known. Were the dreams of evolution true, we should long since have passed earth's formative period, but events of recent years show us that this very globe is going through great and momentous changes, preparatory to the conditions prophesied of for millennial times. Surely never have there been so many terrible disasters on land and sea as since the midnight cry summoned the virgin band to trim their lamps. Earthquakes, tidal waves and kindred phenomena have occurred with amazing frequency. Is it any wonder that we see the sixth sign on every hand? "Men's hearts failing them for fear, and for looking after those things which are coming on the earth." Confidence is shaken. Nations are bewildered and perplexed. Pledges even of nations are violated, and promises broken. Individuals are in fear and dismay where a cheery spirit of optimism prevailed but a short time ago. Yet, amidst it all, the Christian need not be in perplexity or doubt. The Word of God has forewarned of all this. Minutely it has foretold existing conditions, and the fulfilment of its solemn prophecies should only strengthen the faith of the believer as he turns from all men's empty vaporing to the unerring and inerrant Word of God.

This spirit of unrest to which we have referred, is particularly manifested in the strained relations between capital and labor. Despite the evident desire of many modern captains of industry to better the conditions of their employees, and to practise what a recent writer has called "the golden rule in business," capital and labor still maintain a distinctly hostile attitude the one to the other; and the economic questions involved seem no nearer a peaceful and satisfactory solution than in the days when the apostle James wrote his intensely practical epistle.

In that letter there is a passage which, while it unquestionably applied directly to conditions then existing, was so worded by the inspiration of the Holy Spirit as to graphically depict industrial conditions at the end of the age. This is not so manifest on the page of the Authorized Version as in the Revision, or any critical translation. An evidently mistaken rendering of one preposition is responsible for this in the King James Version. This preposition, correctly rendered in later versions, throws a flood of light on the whole passage. It is the word rendered "for" in the earlier translation and "in" in the later ones, occurring in the last sentence of James 5:3. Read the passage in its entirety:

"Come now, ye rich, weep and howl for your miseries that shall come upon you. Your wealth has become corruption, and your garments moth-eaten. Your gold and silver are rusted; and their rust shall be a witness against you, and shall eat your flesh as fire. Ye have heaped up treasure together *in the last days.*" Note the corrected preposition, and observe where in the course of time, it locates the complete fulfilment of that concerning which the Holy Spirit speaks so solemnly. The passage continues: "Behold, the wages of the laborers who have reaped your fields which is of you kept back unjustly, crieth; and the cries of those that have reaped have entered into the ears of the Lord of hosts. Ye have lived in luxury upon the earth, and have been wanton; ye have pampered your hearts [as] in a day of slaughter. Ye have condemned, ye have killed the righteous; he doth not resist you. Be patient therefore, brethren, until the coming of the Lord. Behold, the husbandman waiteth for the precious fruit of the earth, and hath long patience for it, until it receive the early and latter rain. Be ye also patient; establish your hearts, for the coming of the Lord draweth nigh" (5:1– 8, KJV, 1911).

As by a master hand, the apostle with a few bold strokes, pictures the times in which we live. On the one hand, haughty wealth; on the other, grinding poverty; on the one hand, scornful indifference; on the other, angry dissatisfaction. On the one hand, wanton waste; on the other, bitter need. Such contrasts have ever been common in this world's sad history, but never were they so accentuated as at the present time when the rich are growing richer and the poor are growing poorer, and the great gulf between the two classes in steadily widening. Ours has been called, and not without reason, the millionaire age. If our grandfathers were worth a few thousands, they were counted well-to-do. Now men hold securities mounting into the millions, while even a billion of money may be heaped together by one man. Statistics show that the great bulk of the world's wealth is held subject to the order of a little coterie of arrogant plutocrats, who conniving together can control the resources of the nations, and make or prevent financial panics at their will. It is a condition of affairs never before known, and tells us with absolute certainty that we are in the last days.

Nor should I be misunderstood in writing as I have done. It is no sin to be rich, nor is a man necessarily a malefactor because he possesses the ability to amass great wealth. But wealth is a stewardship, and "it is required in stewards that a man be found faithful." He to whom riches are entrusted is accountable to God for the use to which he puts them. Their selfish conservation He will judge unsparingly. James arraigns the rich for their greed and self-indulgence. They had forgotten the word, "He that loveth silver shall not be satisfied with silver; nor he that loveth abundance with increase: this is also vanity" (Eccles. 5:10). They were living as though accountable to no higher power, and were eagerly seeking to gratify every lust. Their hoarded treasure, corrupting, moth-eaten, and rusting, witnessed to their sordid selfishness. And this mass of wealth would soon have been largely dissipated had they but dealt in fairness with the laborers on the fruits of whose toil they were fattening. Those thus downtrodden have often felt as though God had forgotten, and in their despair have often denied His very existence. But "when He maketh inquisition for blood He forgetteth not the cry of the humble." He has been a silent but not unfeeling spectator of the injustice, the heartlessness, and the haughty arrogance of the godless rich. He has noted every tear, heeded every sigh, heard every cry of oppression from the anguished hearts of the downtrodden whose rights have been ruthlessly disregarded by those who should have been to them the instruments of Providence for their protection and blessing. The same spirit that has thus ill-used the poor and needy is the spirit that condemned and slew the Righteous One. It comes to its full fruition in the last days. It will be judged unsparingly when the Lord arises to plead the cause of the afflicted.

But what is to be the Christian's attitude in such conditions as are here described? Is he to link himself with labor unions and industrial associations of various kinds, generally composed of Christless men guilty of violence and even murder, in order to curb the greed and check the tyranny of soulless corporations and capitalists preying on the laboring classes? Is he to oppose force to tyranny, the boycott to oppression, and the strike to employers' arrogance? By no means. His path is indicated clearly and unequivocally in Ecclesiastes 5:7– 12. "The coming of the Lord draweth nigh." Till then the believer is exhorted to patience and to trust in the living God. He is not to be carried away by the spirit of the age. Complaints, grudges, harsh invectives, are not to come from him who sides with a rejected Christ and waits for His return from heaven. Of old, the prophets had to learn this lesson of patience, suffering for righteousness' sake, committing their cause to the Lord; ever proving His faithfulness in spite of all man's unfaithfulness. And they who so endured we count happy, even as was Job the servant of the Lord whose patience has become proverbial, and in whose later history we see "the end of the Lord" and are assured that He is very pitiful and of tender mercy.

Till He comes the Christian can well afford to stand

aside from the restless, surging movements of the day; and, committing his cause to the Lord with quietness of heart, he is to let the potsherds of the earth strive with the potsherds of the earth, knowing that God has said, "I will overturn, OVERTURN, OVERTURN it, until HE shall come, whose right it is to reign." That that glad day has now drawn very near the conditions we have been considering would be sufficient to clearly prove.